1996   W9-AEL-950

Media Events That Shaped the New Croatia

United nations
Transitional
adm in Easter Slovenia

Temple Black

ISBN: 978-0-6151-5837-2

ACKNOWLEDGEMENTS

This book is dedicated to my wife Jeanne Marie. Not only this book, but my U.S. Air Force career would have not been possible without the support, love and understanding of Jeanne and our two daughters, Melissa and Vanessa. For their tireless support over the last 35 years, I salute them and thank them for all they have done to make me a successful military officer, husband and father.

I want to especially acknowledge the outstanding work of the many public affairs practitioners with whom I worked at the UN Mission in Vukovar. The information contained in this book came from our combined experiences, weekly newspapers, television productions, brochures, etc. For all of their outstanding efforts, professionalism and dedication to this important Mission, I salute and thank them.

Croatia

CONTENTS

CHAPTER 1

AN OPPORTUNITY TO EXCEL

It was a cold; wet wintry evening, when I called an old friend --
Jacques Klein. Jacques had been a Pentagon leader during the last part
of the eighties. His position as Secretary of the Air Force for International Affairs was very "high-viz" and powerful in the "Building", referring to the Pentagon, as we liked to say. I was a junior Major, assigned to the Secretary of the Air Force's Office of Public Affairs and
a "watcher"…assigned to help Jacques and his program frame International Affairs issues. If it was good or bad news, I was "in-the-loop".

I developed plans & programs, worked with the staff to develop
THUNDERBIRDS flying schedules, particularly in overseas areas. I
developed concepts to emphasize the great professionalism of the
United States Air Force worldwide. Lt. Colonel's Gary Dills and
Larry Smith were the action officers I worked with every day. Jacques
was always a "wild man" stirring the pot & trying to make things happen. The Secretary of the Air Force at the time was Pete Aldrich.
Jacques and Pete Aldrich got along famously. Aldrich seemed to love
the big bluster and outrageous stories and so he and Klein were buds.
Of course Klein worked hard (and worked his staff hard) to positively
position the Air Force, no matter what the issue.

Jacques was a two-star general in the Air Force Reserves, so he was
attuned to what the active force was doing. He had all the background,

1

and all the schools. He had been a state department guy for thirty-years and as far as I was concerned, was on the leading edge of what was happening worldwide. So, we struck up a friendship. He alone got me promoted to Lieutenant Colonel, after I was passed-over the first time. That was an almost impossible accomplishment and I was deeply appreciative and indebted to him for that.

I had moved on from the Pentagon and Andrews Air Force Base to become Chief of Media Relations at Langley Air Force Base, Virginia...Air Combat Command. While reviewing the morning reports one day, I saw a press clipping showing Jacques had been selected to be the Transitional Administrator for the United Nations in Eastern Slavonia...a place of which I had never heard.

So, that evening I called him. He was in town and I congratulated him on the new appointment. As we talked, he asked what I was doing and I told him I was at Air Combat Command, stationed at Langley. He asked me "How would you like an opportunity to excel?" and if "I wanted to be a part of history?" I said, "well, I've only been on station at Langley for a year and probably couldn't get released." He said "you come with me to Croatia & Serbia and we'll do great things together; see the world, travel & make a great impact on that part of the world." I said I'd have to think about it and he said "don't think too long because we're moving real fast, the trains pulling out of the station and I need an answer quickly". Call me back in a day or two and let me know.

And so I did think about it. I talked to Jeanne (my wife) and explained that the train was on a fast track. It caused some panic because my wife's father had been very sick, had died and we had gone home to New Orleans for the funeral. Since I had only been at Langley for a year, any move required a wavier. Jacques said not to worry about it...if I wanted to go, just say the word and he would get Secretary of State Madeline Albright to ask for me by name for the mission.

So, I decided to go. Both of my daughters, Melissa and Vanessa were off at college and my wife wanted to go back home to be with her mom and reclaim the house we hadn't been in for ten years. But knowing Klein as well as I did, I thought it would be prudent to try and nail him down on a few specifics. So I made my list of what I thought were important questions like "will I be traveling with you to visit the heads of state and the many foreign countries involved? The answer was yes! Will I meet those leaders? Yes! What about the Ambassadors contact Group? How much assistance do you need from the Air Force? Would this duty be in uniform or not? I figured once I had a commitment on these issues, I'd be covered. Wrong again!

He didn't like the questions. They were too specific. But after the conversation I felt I had a handle on the future. Wrong again! I thought I would be traveling the world, doing press conferences, meeting heads of state, saving the world from communism and having a blast. But as we all know, things don't always turn out the way we plan. I also thought this opportunity would lead to a retirement job with the United Nations, since once they saw how great a guy I was, they just wouldn't be able to get along without me. Really, wrong again!

After some deep soul searching, I decided to join the UN mission, thinking it was the right thing to do. I said yes to Jacques...I want to be part of the UNTAES mission in Vukovar, Croatia.

There was something else driving me to go. I had been at Langley for only a year as Chief of Media Relations. I had come to that job from what I consider the best PR job in the Air Force...Director of Public Affairs at Andrews, right outside of Washington. There I had a staff of sixteen great people and over five years of experience, where we garnered great PR for the Air Force. From the war in the Persian Gulf, to interviews of congressional delegations and supporting Air Force One...it was never boring. Doing live "stand-up" interviews on international subjects all the time; working with State Department guys and then with Mike Mc Curry, and Dee Dee Meyer's at the White House; dealing daily with the White House press corps and Chairman of the Joint Chief's of Staff; helping to dispatch the DOD press pool at 3:00

3

AM on some "HOT" breaking news story ...the job at Andrews was a PR guy's "Dream Come True".

That's where I met Roger Ailes, now President of FOX television. One evening, I received a call from Pete Williams's office (Department of Defense Public Affairs) at home saying Roger Ailes would be coming to Andrews and that I should help him as much as I could. Turns out that Roger Ailes ran President George H.W. Bush's presidential campaign and helped get him elected. So, I asked if the Air Force had been notified and was told not to worry about that little detail...just make Mr. Ailes happy.

The next day Bob Gordon showed up (in a long black limousine) saying he worked with Roger and we needed to get started on a two-hour live CBS-TV special. It would happen in about a week, so we had to move quickly. We would be welcoming back the troops from Desert Storm and inviting as many active-duty military and family members as could fit in our biggest hangar. Then Mr. Ailes showed up, and it was easy to see who was running the show. He started asking questions about the countries involved, how many and which ones to invite to participate and I began scrambling, talking to the folks in our International Affairs division. But, that was much too slow, so he asked where the commander's office was. He wanted to "spread out a little". We needed some "working room".

Fortunately my boss, Colonel Jim White, (a hell of a great guy), was out of town and we just swooped into the command section. Ailes asked me to get John Sununu (White House Chief of Staff) on the phone at the White House and he, of course, assumed I had the number. I didn't, but we called information and acted like it was no big deal. I mentioned something like I would be surprised if Mr. Sununu would take the call, but of course, as soon as Ailes identified himself to the White House receptionist, Sununu was on the line. It was obvious that we were on the cutting edge of a very hot project.

We succeeded in getting the project done and it was wonderful. President and Mrs. Bush were the guests of honor at the event and the

President spoke to the troops. I was the MC before the show went live...so that was my 15 minutes of fame! The event was a total success and one I'll always remember.

In the new job at Langley, the volume of work was crushing. While there had been ten action officers working in the section immediately before my arrival, that number was cut to three. Now, of course, you do the best you can and try to cut projects but it's tough to do that when the four-star begins to breathe down your neck. So, the workload increased and the staff support went to zero. It seemed like a lose-lose situation, especially since I had just come from the "Best PR Job in the Air Force".

We went home for the funeral of my father-in-law and the day of the funeral, I received a call from my boss, now Director of Air Force Public Affairs Colonel Ron Rand, asking if I really wanted to take the overseas assignment. He said "you have to make a decision right now if you want this assignment or not". I said, yes I do! He said, OK. You have to be there in about five days. So, at break-neck speed, we returned to Virginia, packed up the house in one day, drove the cars back with Dixie, our miniature Schnauzer, and on April 1, 1996, I left New Orleans for New York, got to Frankfurt and caught a flight to Zagreb, Croatia. I thought I was behind the "power curve" and figured I had to be in-place, like NOW!!! When I got there on April 3rd, I walked in and the staff said, "So who are you?" I said, "Well, I'm Lieutenant Colonel Temple Black and Jacques Klein needs me!!!"

Klein is gone today and we don't know who you are. There are lots of people coming in, so why don't you just go and hang out 'til he returns.

I did just that. I met another military guy, Colonel Jeff Barnett, who was senior to me and was to be the "Commander" but I found out in the first day he had alienated the entire staff, which I thought was very unusual. Turned out there were to be six or seven military folks assigned (all the services involved) and so I went around and started meeting as many of the players as possible. I met Ann Barnes, Klein's secretary. She was wonderful and extremely efficient; Derek Boothby, the British deputy, who was a long-time UN employee, who knew all the ropes and was really there as a company man. I also met a fellow named Phil Arnold—soon to be my nemesis.

Klein had told me I was going to be his spokesman but when I got there, Phil had been appointed as the UN spokesman. So...needless to say, on the first day, we had immediate conflict. I thought I was in-charge; he knew he was in-charge and we had quite a time of it for the first couple of months. I was focused and wanted plans developed to have our senior-leadership agree on a coordinated approach for media relations. Phil was of a different school and focused on different goals...things I really was unaware of at the time. The UN was "different" from the Air Force. There was more of a strong Radio program approach used to attack the Eastern European communist environment, and Phil planned to saturate the population with "The Truth". Then they would be persuaded. I was more into TV communications and immediate feedback, wanting to get a quick feel for the environment in which we were playing.

That evening, Klein returned at about seven o'clock...all hail fellow, well met...and the first thing he said was: "What are you doing here?" Big joke, ha, ha, ha!!! So, we went to dinner with some other folks and ended up at a pizza joint...of all places. That's where I met two of the best, hardest working members of the Mission...U.S. Air Force Major Annie Sumpter and U.S. Air Force Captain Susan Lucas. Annie was assigned as the Mission Historian in order to document what actually happened during our time in Vukovar. This was an extremely important task because as people move on to other assignments, memories get clouded and accomplishments are lost. Because of her great experience and outstanding credentials, we were very fortunate to have Major Sumpter assigned to this important mission.

Susan was slated to be the Executive Officer. She was extremely well organized and focused and along with her strong, vibrant personality was able keep us on track. It would be a difficult task but she handled it with great efficiency and excellent diplomatic aplomb.

Eventually, we ended up at the Intercontinental Hotel, a beautiful place, considering we were supposed to be in a war-zone, where we were billeted for three weeks. And I'm thinking...this isn't half-bad. I'm in a war zone and living in a five-star hotel. Well, one day I got word that we we're moving out and I asked "moving out where?" They said "to the war zone". "War-zone?" I said, Oh No!!! Where's that?

Oh we're going to where the Serbs & Croats are still shooting at each other and where the mass graves are...so get ready!

The UN Headquarters compound was located in downtown Zagreb, Croatia. It was kind of a base point that the UN works out of (a staging area) and this is where I met some of my future best friends in the mission. There was Debra Owens, who had been a long-time UN employee and who on another mission had been shot and almost killed. Her good friend, retired Marine Lieutenant Colonel Buddy Tillet, (I guess there are a lot of us retired types running around), was also to join us in a few weeks. Buddy joined up with a group in New York but he wanted to come and be part of the mission. So, the three of us teamed up and became good friends.

The first day I met Debra, she had a desk, so I knew she was important. I walked in and she had bottles of booze all the way across the desk and the floor and was wearing a designer outfit from Nordstrom's in DC. She was carefully wrapping bottles of liquor and liquors and red & white wine, etc. I said, Debra, "I don't know you but I want to get to know you; what are you doing?" She said, "I'm getting ready for the war!!! This is what you do!!! I asked her "So where did you get the booze?" She said, "I used my ration card". I said "ration card...what's that?" She said, "Oh, you don't know anything, do you?" and I said no. So she took me to meet the ration card guy, since I was only allowed to buy a certain amount of liquor, cigarettes, wine, or beer during the month.

The next day I met would be one to remember because that's when I began to meet the other American military officers assigned to the mission.

CHAPTER 2

THE PLAN

My job was to advise Jacques Klein on the best use of the media to bring the Region under the sovereign control of the Government of Croatia; retain its multiethnic character; promote an atmosphere of confidence among the local residents; enable the refugees and displaced persons to enjoy the right to return freely to their homes; to live there in conditions of security; to promote respect for the highest standards of human rights and freedoms; to promote redevelopment and reconstruction of the Region in harmony with the overall plans of the Republic of Croatia and to organize free and fair local elections not later than 30 days prior to the end of the transitional period.

On the PR side, we had three major components:

1. UNTAES radio employed eleven people and was on the air for seven hours a day.

2. UNTAES television employed seven people and produced a one-hour program three times a week, as well as a one-half hour special program each Saturday at 9:00 pm.

3. UNTAES bulletin was a weekly publication that explained the mission to the public, U.N. military observers and our military

personnel. It was printed in Serbian, Croatian and English and was distributed region wide.

Media relations provided the local population with accurate, current information about the mission. It sought to describe the UNTAES role in facilitating peaceful reintegration.

The target audiences were local, regional, national and international media.

Media Strategy

Long-Term Media Strategy for the United Nations Transitional Administration for Eastern Slavonia, (UNTAES)

1. PURPOSE: to provide guidance, objectives and communications discipline to the Transitional Administration.

2. OBJECTIVES:

A. to introduce and establish the new Transitional Administrator with internal and external publics as the UN's top leader, chief communicator and principal role model

B. to maintain effective communications for the duration of the appointment

C. creates and implements new strategies that uniquely communicated the UNTAES Story to the Region/world.

D. enhance understanding and support of priority issues: i.e. Quality of Life, Modernization, and Leadership

E. foster pride, trust, understanding and confidence in UNTAES

THE PLAN

GOALS:

1 To facilitate the implementation of the agreement in all of its phases.

2. To explain to all peoples of the region the details: the...who, what, when, where, why and how of the implementation plan.

3. To create an atmosphere of confidence and trust-between the two ethnic groups and the Implementation Force

4. Situation:

   a. Background and Facts:

-- Jacques became the United Nations Transitional Administrator on 15 January 1996.

-- There was a requirement, both internally and externally, to explain the mission of UNTAES.

Themes, messages and communications strategies and tactics were intended, to ensure targeted audiences understood the UNTAES vision, mission and values.

   b. Policy: Execution of the plan was in accordance with established UN Public Affairs policies and procedures.

5. Assumptions:

While Public Affairs is the discipline that develops outlet-specific strategies to effectively communicate with publics, it's the Transitional Administrator who establishes and embodies the organization's guiding principles.

b. The Administrator's communications priorities must be established early and spread widely and continuously to all levels of the UN and the mission area.

c. The Administrator must be positioned as a leader with a clear vision, sense of mission, dedication and strong integrity.

d. Competition for the public's attention is intense and their attention span is often short. Communications initiatives must capture their attention and inform them quickly, yet in an understandable manner.

e. Communicating with the UNTAES internal publics was a top priority.

1) UNTAES members were partners in maintaining a clear vision and shared sense of Mission.

2) Successful internal communication hinged on timeliness, credibility, and usefulness.

3.) Credibility was affected by the extent to which the Administrator directly communicated with the internal audience.

f. The plan was not inviolate. Communications themes, messages and initiatives had to be relevant.

g. Two-way feedback was essential to good communications.

6. Audiences:

1) Local population of Eastern Slavonia, Western Sirmium, Baranja and adjoining areas

2) The general population of Croatia.

3) The general population of Serbia.

4) International media in Eastern Slavonia, especially Zagreb and Belgrade.

5) The internal audience of the United Nations organization and various international agencies involved with the implementation force.

6) The general international community.

Methodology:

a) Based on previous UN experiences and local media circumstances, I recommended that messages of the Transitional Administrator be transmitted to the public via radio in a professional, consistent, timely and comprehensive manner.

b) A public radio frequency was secured through regional authorities under complete editorial control of the transitional authority. I had real heartburn with this one-dimensional approach but Phil Arnold, the UN appointed spokesman, was determined to do radio at the expense of any other media, including television. However, he reluctantly agreed to a comprehensive public outreach program with speakers, exhibits, products, printed material, and "open house" visits to contingent troops, etc.

3) Popular handout products were geared to the appropriate audiences. Production design began quickly.

4) Regular weekly newsletters in Serbian, Croatian and English with primary focus on useful information and positive stories.

5) Regular press conferences and planned media activities.

Following below were the activities I wanted Jacques to sign-up to before I devoted a lot of energy on items he wouldn't support. It was tough to nail him down, so he compressed the time for our discussion into a total of five-minutes. I wanted decisions on all of the following topics:

1. Update and print personal biography and get a new official photo.

2. United Nations press service interviews to intro him to the UN family.

3. Develop print and electronic products for UN employees

4. Obtain a news service.

MAJOR ADDRESSES TO UNTAES STAFF

5. Conduct visits with UNTAES Directorates during the first 90 days. Jacques would address top issues and future plans to include present and future; present mission theme, discuss problems. Develop stories as appropriate.

6. Conduct a series of base and deployed-location visits through first 12 months (including three main cities); visits to include built-in time for one or more of the following activities:

1) Meet with Directorate in "Administrator Visits."

2) Newspaper interviews (photos/videotaped) during visits.

3) Brown bag lunch with UNTAES staff

4) Local media availability

6. Meet with UNTAES Public Affairs Staff to discuss communications priorities quarterly.

7. Media skills enhancement session...Media Training. (Jacques looked at me and said..."are you kidding...I know all that stuff").

8. Conduct off-the-record reception in Vukovar to get acquainted with local media.

9. UN magazine interview.

10. Editorial Backgrounder/luncheon/tour of headquarters for International media. Schedule Jacques on "Larry King Live". Discuss the UNTAES mission; field call-in questions from around the world.

11. Conduct media roundtables with Washington DC, New York, Zagreb, Belgrade, etc. correspondents to discuss the progress of the mission.

(It took me at least a week of calling personal contacts in DC to get Jacques set-up with Frank Sesno @ CNN. My pal, Mark Rosenker, an Air Force two-star General and now Chairman of the NTSB, helped me arrange the interview).

12. Administrator's speeches—local, national and international.

13. UNTAES interview on the Lehrer report. Discuss progress of UN mission.

14. Administrator's speech to International Environmental Symposiums.

15. Speech to Major Educational Organization/Universities

16. Discuss building the mission of UNTAES and the regions' future importance.

17. Interviews on CNBC's Equal Time

18. University visit program. Plan a one-hour overview/Q & A with students and one-hour interface with faculty.

19. One church visit per Sunday. Every village had a church, so there were at least 173 opportunities.

MESSAGES:

1. The implementation force will not be an occupational force but is resolved to implement the settlement fully

2. The transitional authority and transitional administration will monitor human rights and the return of refugees.

3. The safety of the Serb population is of utmost importance.

4. Specific messages were to be formulated—in close coordination with other international agencies, NGOs and political authorities— on every aspect of the implementation plan, i.e. human rights monitoring and return of refugees, economic tasks, elections monitoring, police and border monitoring, etc.

MONTHLY RECURRING REQUIREMENTS

UN news service on-the record interviews

Every two months:

- Speech to selected audiences within 150 miles of Vukovar

- Appearances on major network morning talk shows and major market radio talk shows.

- "From the Top" administrator's newsletter

QUARTERLY:

- Select activities in major regions when coincident to UNTAES travel. For example, coordinate an editorial board opportunity with local newspaper reporters, radio/TV interviews, off-the record breakfasts with select civic leaders, larger public-speaking venues, etc.

ANNUALLY:

- Publish a "state of UNTAES mission" report.

- Spend holidays (Thanksgiving, Christmas, etc.) with the UN troops and employees

- Host a national media day. Invite national news leaders to UNTAES.

- Host a civic leader tour, briefings, fact sheets, one hour roundtable meetings with Jacques   and the force commander on current news matters.

- During visits to Washington, conduct on-the record sessions with defense writers groups.

- Speeches to the national press club

- Congressional staff visits

SELECTED EVENTS

- Find issues and public opportunities for Jacques.

- Be visible in all crisis situations.

- Engage critics/opponents of major UNTAES initiatives via personal phone calls and letters-to-editors, op-ed articles, invitations for first-hand looks, background briefings.

- Publish all speeches through UN distribution channels.

- Distribute and market select speeches through computer on-line services, vital speeches, internet, etc.

- Pro-actively address major issues via op-ed articles in major publications.

- When in major media markets, solicit appearances on national talk shows and breakfast programs, i.e. Today Show, Good Morning America, etc.

CHAPTER 3

MESSAGES FOR THE PEOPLE

Following are the messages we developed so that people could begin to understand the situation they were in, the transition taking place and the opportunities they had, if only they would take them. As you can imagine, it's a tough mental and physical transition, going from war to peace.

Question: Will UNTAES protect us from Croatian attack?

Answer: The 5,000 troops of UNTAES are here with a mandate to ensure the security of UNTAES personnel and to contribute, by their presence, to the maintenance of peace and security in the region. In the event of any military threat to the mission, UNTAES has the ability to call on close-air support from NATO.

As the Secretary General's report of 13 December 1995 noted, our military presence is required "not only for demilitarization but also to reassure the inhabitants of the region that, after demilitarization, they will not be exposed to military attack. I believe our presence here provides that added security for the local population.

Furthermore, the transitional administrator has spoken with the Croatian leadership on several occasions and is firmly convinced that no

Croatian police or military action will occur. Such action is clearly not in their interest and would be viewed very seriously by the world community.

War Crimes

Question: Who is authorized to charge people with war crimes?

Answer: The international criminal tribunal for the former Yugoslavia (ICTY) has primacy for all cases of serious violations of international humanitarian law, (including those crimes commonly referred to as "war crimes"), committed on the territory of the former socialist federal republic of Yugoslavia after January 1, 1991. It issues indictments, which are enforceable internationally, and may also issue international arrest warrants. This means that all nations are obligated, if ICTY so requests, to turn over any defendant in a case of this nature. This has been done in a number of cases.

This does not mean that national governments cannot also try individuals suspected of "war crimes." Under the "rules of the road" agreed upon in Rome this year, the governments of Croatia, Serbia and Bosnia and Herzegovina have agreed that such persons would be subjected to criminal proceedings by the government only after it has received clearance from ICTY.

Human Rights: 1 - Post UNTAES

Question: How will our human rights be protected at the end of the UNTAES mandate?

Answer: Under article 10 of the basic agreement, the international community shall monitor and report on respect for human rights in the region on a long-term basis. Article 11 of the basic agreement also requests interested countries and Organizations to monitor and investigate all violations of the agreement and to make appropriate recommendations.

There were many international organizations and NGO's that expressed interest in long-term monitoring of the region. The OSCE had opened an office in Vukovar and UNTAES was coordinating with other organizations. One particularly important organization was the Council of Europe. When Croatia became a member, which was to happen this year, all Croatian citizens would have access to the human rights court in Strasbourg.

The best immediate protection was to be the local police force, which would be comprised of substantial numbers of Serbs. UNTAES had arranged human rights training for not only Serbs but also Croat members of the police force.

Human Rights: 2

Question: Human rights monitoring in other parts of Croatia has been ineffective to prevent persecution of Serbs. How can we trust post-UNTAES monitoring?

Answer: The international community is seriously concerned about human rights violations in other parts of Croatia, particularly in the Krajina region and in western Slavonia. Strong pressure is being placed on the Croatian government to substantially improve its record, and particularly to increase the inadequate police numbers there and to curb the harassment from Croats who are being resettled there from Bosnia and the FRY.

But there are more differences than similarities between this region and the Krajina. Here, a peaceful and orderly reintegration is taking place under the control of the Security Council. Serbs will be involved in all areas of local government of this region including the police. We hope that large numbers of Serbs will stay because there is safety in numbers and no one is sure of how many Croats will return or to where. Moreover, Croatia and the FRY have agreed to mutual protection of minorities, which should give you additional confidence.

Vukovar — war crimes:

Question: When is the international community going to investigate what happened in Vukovar in 1991?

Answer: The UNTAES mandate does not include responsibility for investigating the events of five years ago. The task of investigating any crimes, which may be considered as serious violations of international humanitarian law, rests with the international criminal tribunal for the former Yugoslavia (ICTY).

The presence of UNTAES on the ground provides the secure environment in which international investigators are able to go about their work unmolested. It will be up to them, to collect the evidence and issue indictments against those believed responsible for committing war crimes.

UNTAES supports the position of the international criminal tribunal that there can be no lasting reconciliation among communities until those responsible for crimes are identified and brought to justice. UNTAES will cooperate with ICTY in any way possible, whichever side is involved in the crimes being investigated.

Amnesty law

Question: What is UNTAES doing to bring about a comprehensive amnesty law?

Answer: A comprehensive and clear amnesty law for all those who were not involved in war crimes is essential. The present amnesty law is not sufficient.

Following the secretary-general's June report on the progress of the mission, the security council expressed regret that the Croatian government had not yet taken steps to adopt a comprehensive amnesty law concerning all persons who, either voluntarily or by coercion, had served in the civil administration, military or police forces of the local Serb authorities in the former united nations protected areas, with the exception of those who committed war crimes. The council urged the government to take such action as soon as possible.

UNTAES continues to request the government to enact a comprehensive, clear law. UNTAES has sent to the Croatian government suggested changes to the law. We understand from statements by Croatian officials, including Deputy Prime Minister Kostovic, that the Croatian Sabor will reconsider the amnesty law after it reconvenes. We hope that this renewed discussion will produce a better result.

Autonomy and special status

Question: Why does UNTAES not support autonomy for the region?

Answer: Political autonomy is not a realistic option for this region. Nothing in the UNTAES mandate, neither the basic agreement signed in Erdut or the UN Security Council resolutions, stipulates the establishment of any special political status or autonomy for the region. The internationally recognized position is that the region is an integral part of the republic of Croatia and thus fully subject to Croatian law. The issue of autonomy was not even included in the normalization of relation's agreement between Croatia and the FRY.

UNTAES does not put ideas on autonomy or special status forward because it is not part of our mandate to alter the arrangements fixed by the parties in the basic agreement. Our job is to do all that we can so that the residents of the region, as citizens of Croatia, enjoy the whole scope of internationally recognized human rights and freedoms. In this regard, we will work with the local population and the Croatian government to ensure that the cultural, educational, religious and employment rights of all are equally respected.

Elections

Question: How will we be able to vote to elect our own representatives in the elections?

Answer: At least one month before its departure, elections will be organized by UNTAES for all local government bodies. An internationally recognized expert from the United Nations electoral division is commencing work in September to plan and organize the elections, which will be held in accordance with the highest international standards.

The date and modalities of the elections have not yet been settled. The arrangements will be determined in consultation with the Croatian government and the elections will be conducted under the supervision of UNTAES, OSCE and other international organizations.

Full participation in the elections by all inhabitants of the region is the best guarantee of proportional representation in the local government bodies which will administer the area after UNTAES leaves.

Return of displaced Serbs

Question: What is UNTAES doing to make it possible for displaced Serbs to return to their own homes in other parts of Croatia?

Answer: The Croatian government has repeatedly stated that all Croatian citizens have the right to live wherever they choose in Croatia. This is a fundamental right, which is guaranteed under the constitution. The Erdut agreement provides specifically that all persons have the right to return to their places of residence in the region and to live there in security. The agreement also provides that all persons who have come to the region and who had previous permanent residence elsewhere in Croatia have the right to live in the region.

UNHCR, not UNTAES, is the lead agency in assisting the return of displaced persons to their homes in western Slavonia and elsewhere in Croatia. The mandate of UNTAES only covers this region. UNTAES is working very closely with UNHCR to implement a program which includes both the return of Serb displaced persons to their homes outside the region and the return of Croatians to their homes within the region and has assisted several Serbs to return to their homes outside the region.

The Croatian government is well aware that Serbs must be able to move out of Croat homes if Croats are to return to the region. A guiding principle is that no one will be turned out of accommodation and left without shelter.

Currency

Question: Do we have to accept the Kuna as our currency?

Answer: The Kuna is the official currency of Croatia, and the territory under UNTAES administration is recognized as an integral part of the republic of Croatia. Therefore, the Kuna will be the legal currency in this area.

If using the Kuna enables you to get the best price for your products and to buy the things you want, it would be foolish not to use it.

We expect that as Kuna become more common in circulation, it will be easier to find stores, which accept it. It can already be used at the UNTAES markets every Saturday. We expect that banks and exchange facilities will soon be established here to enable you to freely convert Kuna, Dinar, Deutch mark and dollars. This is a common practice throughout the world.

Telephone threats

Question: Why are the telephone lines left on when they are used to make threats to people in the region? What is UNTAES doing to end this harassment?

Answer: The reestablishment of direct telephone links has been one step toward peaceful reintegration. It would be a step backwards if the phone lines were disconnected and people were no longer able to make contact with their family and friends.

Unfortunately, one of the consequences of this is that some people have been using the phone lines to harass people. This is happening from both sides, but is limited to extremists. But many constructive contacts and dialogues are also being held.

The transitional administrator has raised this problem at the highest levels with the Croatian government, which deplores these harassing telephone calls.

Investment and economic aid

Question: UNTAES said it will contribute to the economic development of the region, but we have seen nothing. When will investment and development begin?

Answer: UNTAES has put a great deal of effort into developing assistance projects. Unfortunately, many of these projects have taken months to move from the proposed stage to actual implementation. But the first assistance and aid projects are now under way.

As for business investment, such projects will likely take longer. One reason for this is that investors will wait until the legal environment is clear. Before putting much money into a new business, or rebuilding an old business, in the region, an investor will want to know what commercial laws and regulations apply, and how the local authorities, including the courts, will treat his or her business. In the end, it is clear, that the applicable law will be Croatian law, but the process of reintegration must progress before all Croatian commercial law can be applied in the region.

The first new investment will likely come from Croatian companies, especially those restarting facilities they may have had in the area before the war. One example is the oil company, INA, which already has plans for new equipment and investment at Djeletovci oil field. INA has already signed employment contracts with over 90 employees who are resident in the region to work at the oil field.

Damaged property/reconstruction assistance

Question: What can I do to repair or get compensation for property which was destroyed, damaged or stolen during the war?

Answer: The basic agreement states that "the right to recover property, to receive compensation for property that cannot be returned, and to receive assistance in reconstruction of damaged property shall be equally available to all persons." This is an important issue, because we know that many homes were destroyed in the war. We are in the process of finding international donors to assist in reconstruction, but we do not have any projects underway yet.

The Croatian government also has programs for aiding in the reconstruction of damaged property. This aid is only available to citizens of Croatia, however. Whether and how such aid will be made available to residents of the region who are not ethnic Croats, or who did not leave the region during the war, is still not clear. Firm answers to this question will have to come from the Croatian ministry for reconstruction.

Education

Question: Will children be able to attend schools that teach in their mother tongue and alphabet? Will alternative curriculum from the standard Croatian curriculum be available in subjects where perspectives may vary with ethnicity, such as history or literature?

Answer: The basic agreement states that the highest levels of internationally recognized human rights and fundamental freedoms shall be respected in the region. As regards education, these human rights include the right to education and use of the mother tongue.

Visits

Question: How can I, as a displaced Croat, visit my home or village within the region?

Answer: We will facilitate visits to your hometown communities as soon as physically possible. We expect those visits to take place in the very near future.

Question: How can I, as a displaced Serb, visit my home elsewhere in Croatia?

Answer: We are working as fast as we can to make such visits occur. We expect to visit your home areas in the very near future.

Question: How can I see my relatives on the other side?

Answer: Because of limited resources, UNTAES is generally only able to arrange family visits in cases of urgent humanitarian need, particularly weddings, funerals, or in cases of terminal illness. For these visits to be arranged you need to contact the nearest UNTAES civil affairs office. They are located in Ilok, Vinkovci, Vukovar, Osijek, Erdut, and Beli Manastir.

For other cases of family meetings, ICRC organizes family reunions at sites in the former zone of separation.

Documentation

Question: How can I get Croatian documents?

Answer: We are planning to open "one stop shops" inside the region staffed by Croatian government officials, beginning on August 20th. The first office will be in Beli Manastir, with others opening in Ilok and Vukovar soon thereafter. Officials from the Croatian Ministry of Interior, Ministry of Administration will staff them for displaced persons and refugees. They will issue Domovnica (citizenship certificates), identity cards and other related personal documents. They should also be able to address other issues such as pensions. The planned hours of business will be Tuesday, Wednesday and Thursday from 0900 to 1400 hours.

The civil rights project located in Vukovar at Dalmatinska also assists with documentation and issues regarding property.

Question: Will my current identity documents and other personal documents still be valid?

Answer: Authorities outside of the Region do not accept local identity documents as valid, except in some cases in Yugoslavia. As far as UNTAES is concerned, taking Croatian documents will not affect the validity of other personal documents currently held (drivers license, etc.) How Croatian authorities will treat other personal documents such as birth, marriage or death certificates after the transitional period has yet to be fully determined.

Pensions

Question: Will the Croatian government pay my pension?

Answer: The Croatian government has begun a pilot project in Darda where they are paying nearly two hundred pensions. They have now paid these pensions two times, for July and August. The Croatian government is responsible for this issue; UNTAES is only assisting in arranging the payments. The Croatian government has so far said that it will only pay pensions to individuals who have received their Domovnica. They also are only paying the current monthly amounts. No decision that we know of has been made regarding pensions that may have been owed during the last five years. The pension payments are made in Kuna.

Mandate

Question: How long will the UNTAES mandate last?

Answer: The basic agreement states that the transitional period shall be 12 months, "which may be extended to another 12 months if requested by one of the parties."

The local regional council has requested an extension of the transitional period and the UNTAES mandate to 15 January 1998. The Croatian government has said that UNTAES should conclude its current mandate on 15 January 1997, with a more limited mandate being approved for a further few months.

The final decision on the length of the UNTAES mandate rests with the U.N. Security Council, which has "affirmed its readiness to consider, at an appropriate time, extending the duration of the mandate of UNTAES, on the basis of the basic agreement, its resolution 1037 (1996), and a recommendation from the Secretary-General."

In his monthly report on UNTAES of 6 August 1996, the Secretary General noted, "It does not appear realistic to expect that these tasks (of its mandate) will be completed by the expiration of the current UNTAES mandate." The Security Council will have to decide on any extension of the UNTAES mandate prior to 15 January 1996 but it is not possible to say at this time when such a decision will be made, and what that decision will be.

Weapons registration

Question: With the completion of the demilitarization period, how do we register weapons? What happens if we have an unregistered weapon?

Answer: The only weapons, which anyone present in the region may have, are those, which have been properly registered with UNTAES. All persons should immediately register any weapons they have at the nearest Transitional Police Force (TPF) station. TPF officers at all stations have been trained and supplied with forms to register weapons. Possessing an unregistered weapon can lead to the confiscation of the weapon, substantial fines, and even imprisonment.

Only personal and hunting weapons can be registered. All other weapons, such as automatic weapons (Kalashnikov), semiautomatic weapons with cartridges of 10 rounds or more or explosive weapons should be turned in at an UNTAES base or TPF station or else removed from the region.

Other conditions for registering a weapon are that the owner must be 18 years of age or older, be in good mental and physical health, not have been convicted of a crime, and have a justifiable reason for possessing the weapon.

No weapons, not even those, which have been registered, may be carried in public. Possessing a weapon outside the home, with the exception of hunting or sport weapons being used for that purpose within a 10 km radius of one's home, can result in confiscation of the weapon and other penalties.

Impermissible weapons/weapons buy-back

Question: Are you saying that if I own a weapon such as a Kalashnikov there is no way I can keep it? I just have to give it for free to UNTAES? Won't there be a program to buy weapons back from the population?

Answer: You may not legally possess a weapon such as a Kalashnikov, or a mortar, within the Region. At present, you have two options. You can turn it in to an UNTAES base, where it will be destroyed, or you can remove the weapon from the region entirely. There may be a weapons buy-back program in the future, but no final decision has been made on what type of program might be adopted. In the meantime, UNTAES has every right to confiscate any unregistered weapon we find without providing any compensation.

CHAPTER 4

THE KEYS TO MISSION SUCCESS

When I arrived in Vukovar, I was shocked by the devastation and bombed-out buildings I saw. Everywhere I went there was rubble. I was able to get to the compound and find the temporary buildings where our operations would be held. I was fortunate because someone was assigned from the UN to help new people find accommodations. I visited a home that had more bullet holes than any house in a five-mile area. Since it was such a great conversation piece, I decided to take it. At least I had a place to sleep…and it was only three houses away from my new found friends, Buddy Tillett and Deborah Owens.

The next day I went to work and found a few people in the Public Information Office. We discussed how to communicate with the public and reviewed the use of radio, TV and print. We decided that beginning with a print product was the way to go.

We drafted our first article addressing the concepts of reintegrating and reconciling. The key to the success of the UN Transitional Administration for Eastern Slavonia, Baranja and Western Sirmium lay in the reintegration of the region into the Croatian Republic and reconciliation of the various ethnic groups. We announced plans for implementing resolution 1037, adopted by the Security Council, establishing the United Nations Transitional Administration in Eastern Slavonia (UNTAES), which had a 12-month mandate and was comprised of military and civilian components. The Transitional Administrator was authorized to govern the area and be the final arbiter of any disputes in all aspects of this complex task.

Careful not to underestimate the difficulty of reconciling ethnic groups, which had fought over the region for four years, we foresaw no major military problems. We believed the military component of UNTAES, backed by a planned UN Civilian Police presence of 600 monitors, and a team of UN Civil Affairs and Information personnel, would be able to build security and confidence and help the population concentrate on the main job of rebuilding railways, roads and reestablishing postal, telephone, telegraph, customs and educational facilities.

While negotiations with potential troop-contributing Governments continued in New York and in National capitals, the Belgian and Russian troops who had patrolled Eastern Slavonia since 1992 remained in place and continued with their task of maintaining stability along the zone separating the Croatian Army and the Serb military forces. With an authorized initial deployment of 5,000 troops, we believed we had enough soldiers to provide the security necessary to carry out disarmament, once the force was fully in place. To this end, we planned to deploy mechanized, mobile personnel who would have high visibility as they went about their tasks, thus helping boost the confidence of local civilians. The 30-day period allowed for disarmament would commence once the UNTAES military commander certified that all resources were in place. Our goal was that within a year or so, we would be able to stand on the border between Croatia and the Federal Republic of Yugoslavia and Hungary and it would be open to travel, commerce and trade...open to reintegration into Europe. Then we could say our mission was complete, we would lower the flag and go home.

Resolution 1037

Following are the main points of Security Council Resolution 1037, which pertained to the UN peacekeeping operation in Eastern Slavonia, Baranja and Western Sirmium:

The Security Council, determined to ensure the security and freedom of movement of personnel of the United Nations peace-keeping operation in the Republic of Croatia, and to that end, acting under

Chapter VII of the Charter of the United Nations:

1. Decided to establish for an initial period of 12 months, a United Nations peacekeeping operation for the Region, referred to in the Basic Agreement, with both military and civilian components, under the name "United Nations Transitional Administration for Eastern Slavonia, Baranja and Western Sirmium" (UNTAES)

2. Requested the Secretary-General to appoint, in consultation with the parties and with the Security Council, a Transitional Administrator, who had overall authority over the civilian and military components of UNTAES, and who exercised the authority given to the Transitional Administration in the Basic Agreement

3. Decided the demilitarization of the Region, as provided in the Basic Agreement, be completed within 30 days from the date the Secretary-General informed the Council, based on the assessment of the Transitional Administrator the military component of UNTAES was deployed and ready to undertake its mission

4. Requested the Secretary-General to report monthly to the Council, the first such report to be submitted within one week after the date on which the demilitarization was completed

5. Strongly urged the parties to refrain from any unilateral action which could hinder the hand-over from UNCRO to UNTAES or the implementation of the Basic Agreement and encouraged them to continue to adopt confidence-building measures to promote an environment of mutual trust

6. Decided that, no later than 14 days after the date on which demilitarization was scheduled to be completed, it would review whether the

parties had shown a willingness to implement the Basic Agreement, taking into consideration the parties' actions and information provided to the Council by the Secretary-General

It decided to reconsider the mandate of UNTAES if at any time it received a report from the Secretary-General that the parties had significantly failed to comply with their obligations under the Basic Agreement.

The resolution requested the Secretary-General to report to the Council no later than 15 December 1996 on UNTAES and the implementation of the Basic Agreement and expressed its readiness to review the situation in light of that report and to take appropriate action. It decided that the military component of UNTAES consists of a force with the initial deployment of up to 5,000 troops, which had the following mandate:

To supervise and facilitate the demilitarization as undertaken by the parties to the Basic Agreement, according to the schedule and procedures established by UNTAES;

To monitor the voluntary and safe return of refugees and displaced persons to their home of origin in cooperation with the United Nations High Commissioner for Refugees, as provided in the Basic Agreement;

To contribute, by its presence, to the maintenance of peace and security in the region and otherwise assist in implementation of the Basic Agreement;

Decided that, consistent with the objectives and functions set out in the Secretary-General's report of December 13, 1995, the civilian component of UNTAES had the following mandate:

a) Establish a temporary police force, define its structure and size, develop a training program, oversee its implementation, and monitor treatment of offenders and the prison system, as quickly as possible

b) Undertake tasks relating to civil administration.

c) Undertake tasks relating to the functioning of the public services

d) Facilitate the return of refugees.

e) Organize elections, to assist in their conduct, and to clarify the results.

f) Undertake other activities described in the Secretary-General's report, including assistance in the coordination of plans for the development and economic reconstruction of the Region

Decided that UNTAES would monitor the parties' compliance with their commitment, as specified in the Basic Agreement, to respect the highest standards of human rights and fundamental freedoms,

Promote an atmosphere of confidence among all local residents irrespective of their ethnic origin, monitor and facilitate the de-mining of territory within the region, and maintain an active public affairs element.

Called upon the Government of the Republic of Croatia to include UNTAES and the United Nations liaison Office in Zagreb in the definition of "United Nations Peace Forces and Operations in Croatia" in the Status of Forces Agreement with the United Nations and requested the Secretary-General to confirm urgently, on whether this had been done.

Decided that Member States, acting nationally or through regional organizations or arrangements, may, at the request of UNTAES and on the basis of procedures communicated to the United Nations, take all necessary measures, including close air support, in defense of UN-TAES and, as appropriate, assist in the withdrawal of UNTAES;

Requested that UNTAES and the multinational implementation force (IFOR) authorized by the Council in resolution 1031 (1995) of 15 December 1995 cooperate, as appropriate, with each other, as well as with the High Representative;

Called upon the parties to the Basic Agreement to cooperate with all agencies and organizations assisting in the activities related to implementation of the Basic Agreement, consistent with the mandate of UNTAES;

Requested all international organizations and agencies active in the Region to coordinate closely with UNTAES; Called on States and international financial institutions to support and cooperate with efforts to promote the development and economic reconstruction of the Region;

Underlined the relationship between the parties of their commitments in the Basic Agreement and the readiness of the international community to commit financial resources for reconstruction and development;

Reaffirmed that all States cooperate fully with the International Tribunal for the Former Yugoslavia and its organs in accordance with the provision of resolution 827 (1993) of 25 May 1993 and the, Statute of the International Tribunal and comply with the requests for assistance or orders issued

Stressed that UNTAES would cooperate with the International Tribunal in the performance of its mandate, including with regard to the prosecution of the sites identified by the Prosecutor and persons conducting investigations for the International Tribunal;

22. Requested the Secretary-General to submit for consideration by the Council at the earliest possible date a response on the possibilities for

contributions from the host country in offsetting the costs of the operation;

23. Decided to remain actively engaged in this matter.

Points of the Basic Agreement

The parties agreed as follows:

There was a transitional period of 12 months, which could be extended to another 12 months if requested by one of the parties.

The UN Security Council established a Transitional Administration, which governed the Region during the transition period in the interest of all persons resident in or returning to the Region.

The UN Security Council authorized an international force to deploy during the transitional period to maintain peace and security in the Region and otherwise to assist in implementation of this Agreement. The Region was demilitarized according to the schedule and procedures determined by the International force. The demilitarization had to be completed not later than 30 days after deployment of the International force and included all military forces, weapons, and police, except for the international force and for police operating under the supervision of, or with the consent of the Transitional Administration.

The Transitional Administration ensured the possibility for the return of refugees and displaced persons to their homes of origin. All persons who had left the Region or who had come to the Region with previous permanent residence in Croatia were to enjoy the same rights as all other residents of the Region. The Transitional Administration also took steps necessary to re-establish the normal functioning of all public services in the Region without delay.

The Transitional Administration helped to establish and train temporary police forces, build professionalism among the police and confidence among all ethnic communities.

The highest levels of internationally recognized human rights and fundamental freedoms were respected in the Region.

All persons had the right to return freely to their place of residence in the Region and to live there in conditions of security. All persons who left the Region or who had come to the Region with previous permanent residence in Croatia had the right to live in the Region.

All persons had the right to have restored to them any property that was taken from them by unlawful acts or that they were forced to abandon and to just compensation for property that could not be restored.

The right to recover property, to receive compensation for property that could not be returned, and to receive assistance in reconstruction of damaged property was equally available to all persons without regard to ethnicity.

Interested countries and organizations were requested to take appropriate steps to promote the accomplishment of the commitments in this Agreement. After the expiration of the transition period, consistent with established practice, the international community monitored and reported on respect for human rights in the Region on a long-term basis.

Not later than 30 days before the end of the transitional period, elections for all local government bodies, including for municipalities, districts, and counties, as well as the right of the Serbian community to appoint a joint Council of municipalities, had to be organized by the Transitional Administration. International organizations and institutions (e.g. the Organization for Security and Cooperation in Europe, the United Nations) and interested states were requested to oversee the elections.

The Government of the Republic of Croatia was required to cooperate fully with the Transitional Administration and the international force. During the transitional period the Croatian Government authorized the presence of international monitors along the international border of the Region in order to facilitate free movement of persons across existing border crossings.

The Agreement entered into force upon the adoption by the UN Security Council.

It was signed on November 12, 1995 by: Mr. Milan Milanovich, Head, Negotiating Delegation, Mr. Hrvoje Sarinic, Head, Croatian Government Negotiating Delegation and was witnessed by: Mr. Peter Galbraith, United States Ambassador & Mr. Thorwald Stoltenberg, United Nations representative.

Four Weapons Collection Points

"Four weapons collection points were set up under the demilitarization plan for Eastern Slavonia and all heavy weapons had to be destroyed or made unusable once they were handed in", said UNTAES Force Commander, Major-General Joseph Schoups. General Schoups, of Belgium, said the collection points would be located in four areas of responsibility of UNTAES, which included Belgian, Russian, Jordanian and Pakistani troops.

UN Military Observers monitored the return of the weapons, which was a major condition of the Basic Agreement signed by the Head of the Croatian Government Delegation, and the Head of the Serb Negotiating Delegation, on November 12, 1995.

"We expected the weapons to be brought in voluntarily, but tried to convince people that they must cooperate," said General Scoops, who served as Deputy Commander of Belgium's Interservice Territorial Command before taking up his new post with UNTAES.

The demilitarization had to be completed not later than 30 days after deployment of the international force and include military forces, weapons, and police, except for the international force and the police operating under the supervision, or with the consent of the Transitional Administrator. The full deployment of 5,000 UNTAES troops was completed at the end of April. General Scoops said demilitarization would start "after all the necessary conditions for the operation were in place and he had consulted with the Transitional Administrator to set a suitable date".

Among the heavy weapons we had an estimated 100 tanks and 150 artillery pieces in the region, he said.

"Collecting small arms such as rifles, pistols and grenades was more difficult because they could be hidden," said Schoups. "We would not store any of the weapons. We destroyed them by taking them to an area and making them unusable." General Schoups said after the 30-day demilitarization period, we would assess whether there had been enough cooperation from the sides to allow the operation to continue.

"This was a significant moment, which was carefully scrutinized by the Security Council," he said.

In maintaining peace and security after demilitarization was completed, UNTAES troops controlled all checkpoints, conducted patrols and maintained a strong presence along the boundaries of the former Sector East. These boundaries included what used to be the former zone of separation between the sides.

"We created a climate of confidence among the local communities," said General Schoups. "Our troops were actively displayed and integrated closely with the people, getting to know them and to understand their needs." UNTAES troops played an important role in supervising the demining of the Region by the Croats and the Serbs.

Scoops said UNTAES would monitor and assist the return of refugees and displaced persons to the region, providing protection and security to the maximum extent possible. As to the use of close air support for the defense of UNTAES, General Schoups said he would call in NATO close air support when the security of UNTAES was seriously threatened or when major problems arose concerning freedom of movement.

"We had a mission of demilitarization," he said. "The region was kept demilitarized and we were present around the region. And close air support was the visible and real link between this operation and IFOR."

Civilian Police Start Joint Patrols

The start of joint patrolling by the UN Civilian Police (CivPol) and local Police in Eastern Slavonia marked an important step forward in the implementation of the Basic Agreement. By mid-February, there was a close working relationship between Civ Pol and the Militias, which gave the Civilian Police a highly visible profile in the community as they went about their work. This in turn helped engender trust between the Serb population and the Transitional Administration, thus preparing the way for larger steps and greater confidence that was required in the months ahead as the disarmament, repatriation and election process unfolded.

"Two months ago, we had no basis for getting patrols to work," said the Civ Pol Commissioner, Hakan Jurors, of Sweden. "Things developed very rapidly and we're getting excellent cooperation from the Militias. Things are definitely moving in the right direction."

More than 100 of the planned 600 CivPol monitors were deployed in the area. They covered both the northern and southern parts of the region, being based close to the Militias in their stations in Bali Manastir. Other monitors were training in Zagreb and being deployed progressively to the Region.

Meanwhile, those operating from Dali and Bali Manastir worked in teams in defined geographic areas, so as to cover as much ground as possible. The four teams working out of the Dali station, for example, covered the Dali, Vukovar and Ilok areas while from Bali Manastir three teams covered the neighboring region, including liaison with the Militia station at Darda and Batina. Patrols were undertaken both by car and on foot, to enable the CivPol officers to get to know the communities among which they were living. Patrolling was limited to set periods each day, but once the resources were in place, liaison with the Militia was available 24 hours a day.

Mission Facts: Deployment as of 1 March 1996:

Belgian Battalion	683
Russian Battalion	948
Slovak Eng. Battalion	587
Military Observers	100
Civilian Police	103

Planned Deployment:

Military	5000
Military Observers	100
Civilian Police	600
International Civilians	469
Locally recruited civilians	681
Total	6,850

Civilian Population of the Region:

Now estimated (1996)	160,000-170,000
Pre-war estimated	190,000-200,000

44

Ethnic Composition:

Est. 92% Serb
Est. 8% Other

UNHCR Beneficiaries:

Approximately 78,000 were displaced.

Families meet after three year separation

Dusica felt her heart pounding as the UN bus carrying her and 35 other people approached the Sans-Nemetin crossing in the former zone of separation in Eastern Slavonia. She had convinced herself that she was about to experience a dream. The bus passed the Serb-controlled checkpoint and entered a neutral area. Another UN bus had brought in people from the Croatian side. Anxious eyes sought out their family members from among the crowd in tents rigged up by the UN. As people rushed towards each other with out-stretched arms, UN military personnel turned away to hide their tears, as sobbing people hugged and kissed each other.

That day, Dusica finally met her daughter after three years of separation. Regular family reunions began after October 1995. More than 1,100 people met their family members or friends at the Sans-Nemetin checkpoint.

Organizing reunions required a lot of preparation and coordination with the various bodies involved. People who wished to meet with their families from the "other side" first had to approach local Red Cross representatives to register. Lists were then exchanged to trace people and obtain their consent.

Transportation from the Croatian side was easily organized with UN help. On the Serb side, however, people relied on the UN to transport them to the meeting point. The meetings generally lasted for about two hours and people were allowed to carry food and other items. Efforts were made to hold reunions in Bilge to enable families meet each other.

Deployment of Military Observers

Plans for the demilitarization of Eastern Slavonia received a boost in February of 1996 with the deployment of the first of an authorized 100 United Nations Military Observers (UNMOs). The unarmed UNMOs brought to bear a wide range of experience gained in the region over the past number of years. Their tasks were clearly specified by the Secretary-General in a letter to the Security Council on January 26th. "Our main task was to identify all units and equipment to be demilitarized, to monitor the process of demilitarization and at the same time report any developments on the ground which were relevant to maintaining stability and security in the region," said the UNMO Chief Operations Officer, Lieutenant-Colonel Victor Tarusin. "We were not tasked to carry out demilitarization ourselves. That was the job of the battalions. UNMO's are monitors, and as monitors we assisted the implementation forces with our knowledge and liaison capabilities, and helped establish normal relations between the new troops who are arriving and the local commanders, to build understanding and confidence."

Security Council resolution 1043 authorized the UNMO deployment for an initial period of six months. The UNMOs operated in six teams inside the region, from Beli Manastir, Darda, Dalj, Bobota, Negoslavci and Sotin. Later they expected to deploy from Voinovich and Osijek, because they were allowed to operate west of the former zone of separation, placing them technically outside the region. A team was already in place in Osijek ready to begin patrolling. Under arrangements worked out with the Croatian Government, up to 25 UNMOs were to be stationed outside the region and 75 inside.

With the setting up of separate UN missions in Prevlaka, Eastern Slavonia, Bosnia and Herzegovina and the Former Yugoslav Republic of Macedonia, the former centralized UNMO Headquarters in Zagreb was reduced to the status of a liaison office. It handled the arrival of new officers in each of these missions except in Bosnia and Herzegovina, which no longer had UNMOs. The UNTAES UNMOs were fully operational by April, 1996.

CHAPTER 5

GUARANTEED SAFETY & HUMAN RIGHTS

The Croatian Government had given a formal undertaking to the Council of Europe that it intended to take all necessary measures to guarantee the safety and human rights of the Serb population of Croatia, particularly those in the former United Nations Protected Areas. The undertaking, set out in a document signed on 15 March by President Franjo Tudjman and the President of the Sabor, Vlatko Pavletic, formed part of a 21-point declaration, which the Croatian Government had forwarded to the Council of Europe in support of Croatia's bid for membership on the Council. The document declared that Croatia would "take all necessary measures, including adequate police protection, to guarantee the safety and human rights of the Serb population in Croatia, in particular in the former UN Protected Areas, to facilitate the return of people who left those areas and to allow them, through a specific procedure established by law, to effectively exercise their rights to recover property or receive compensation ".

The declaration also committed Croatia to comply strictly with its obligations under the Basic Agreement on the Region of Eastern Slavonia, Baranja and Western Sirmium and to cooperate fully with the UN Transitional Administration for the Region (UNTAES). Croatia had also undertaken to cooperate fully and effectively in the implementation of the Dayton-Paris Agreement for peace in Bosnia and Herzegovina; to cooperate with, and actively assist, the Prosecutor of the International Criminal Tribunal for the former Yugoslavia in bringing before the Tribunal, without delay, persons indicted for war crimes, crimes against humanity and genocide; and to settle outstanding international border disputes according to the principles of international law. The Political Committee of the Parliamentary Assembly of the Council of Europe voted on 17 March to support Croatia's membership of the Council. Two further Committees were scheduled to consider the application before it passed to the Assembly and finally the Council of Ministers in early May.

Recognizing the importance of religion among the people of Eastern Slavonia, Baranja and Western Sirmium, Transitional Administrator (TA) Jacques Klein paid his respects to the main religious leaders of the Region and visited their respective houses of worship during several of his recent visits. While in Eastern Slavonia, he met Orthodox Bishop Lukijan of Dalj, and Father Marko, of the Catholic Church in Ilok. In Baranja, he attended services in the Orthodox Church in Beli Manastir and the Hungarian Catholic church in Knezevi Vinogradi. His message to all the religious leaders he met, and their congregations, was the same. He told them that it was his firm intention, through the authority vested in him as TA for implementing the UNTAES mandate, to make it possible for all people who will make their home in the Region to practice their chosen religion(s) in conditions of freedom and security.

At the same time, Jacques expressed the hope that Church leaders, as respected figureheads in their communities, would play a positive role in helping create the kind of atmosphere in which peace could take root. Freedom of religion is guaranteed in the United Nations Universal Declaration of Human Rights. For Easter, special church services were held in Ilok on April 7 and were planned for Dalj on April 14. Both were expected to be attended by members of different religious communities, as well as representatives from embassies and the UN. I remember being a team member on the Ukrainian helicopter and landing in an elementary schools soccer field. It was strange having all the Ambassadors on board the helicopter, all in one place. I thought…what an opportunity for an ambush. Also, with the contact group together on the aircraft, I wondered what would happen if the helicopter crashed and wiped all of us out. Fortunately, that didn't happen and we landed safely. There was however, a great deal of disagreement between Derek Boothby, the deputy and Jacques on "pushing the envelope" too far…too quickly. Everything was a fight. So, to those who think politics is an easy life, I would say they don't know what they're talking about.

The key task facing UNTAES was to promote an atmosphere of confidence among local residents, thereby preserving the multiethnic character of the Region. What we were trying to do is improve the quality of the lives of the people living here. We were saying: the war is over, we're here to help you through the transition, and the future will be better than the past. Overcoming the doubts, fears and inbuilt prejudices would, nevertheless, not be easy, in part because both sides had heavily propagandized their populations, for their own reasons. "What we produced was honest information, so that we educated the population about the changes that were taking place. The media in general needed to be more honest, and we in UNTAES promised to report things accurately and not distort statements. We were on the radio, distributing our newsletter and remained open to the public." UNTAES developed the process of putting together the military structure needed to make the transition flow smoothly. Once the Jordanian and Pakistani mechanized infantry battalions arrived, UNTAES with the Russian, Belgian and Slovak Battalions already in place, we had the military resources necessary to proceed to the demilitarization phase. After that, the civilian phase of the recovery gathered momentum". That meant the economic recovery of the region, creating jobs and bringing in investment continued to grow. We were encouraged by the commitment of Presidents Tudjman and Milosevic to this peaceful reintegration.

Sowing the Seeds of Harmony

With winter drawing to a close, the question uppermost in the minds of farmers in the Region related to the spring sowing. Most of the inhabitants earned their living through farming, and the area was one of the most fertile in former Yugoslavia. Because of this, UNTAES gave top priority to the Joint Implementation Committee (JIC) on Agriculture, a body set up to find solutions acceptable to both sides on farming matters in the short and medium term. The first meeting of this Committee was mediated by UNTAES on February 1 at the Sarvas-Nemetin crossing, within the Zone of Separation. Representatives of both sides were urged to consider the fixing of the agenda, venue and frequency of future meetings. At that meeting, the participants agreed to meet every Thursday at the crossing point and the Croatian delegation indicated the readiness of the Croatian Government to include the Region in its annual budget, to ensure equitable access to Croatian funding.

The participants were all experts in their respective fields and the meetings were generally held in a cordial atmosphere, with both sides displaying an eagerness to cooperate on concrete plans of action. After the first session, seven additional meetings were held. Such was the degree of confidence that during the meeting on March 14, both delegations decided to dispense with the buses and security escorts provided by the UN and to use their own transport to reach the venue. An in-principle agreement was also reached to hold future meetings outside the Zone of Separation.

While the main committee discussed issues related to spring planting, two subcommittees were established to focus on veterinary and environmental matters and water regime regulations. The Serb side was asked to submit its requirements concerning mobile water pumps and rat extermination pesticides to the UNHCR office in Erdut. Significant progress had been made on several points of common understanding, and the Croatian side came up with an offer of possible financing for the spring planting of sugar beet, sunflowers and corn. The produce harvested on the basis of this finance was processed outside the Region, its value to be assessed on the basis of uniform prices prevailing throughout Croatia. The value of the offer was in the area of 1.6 million deutschmarks and was a forerunner of other transactions of mutual benefit, representing a major step in confidence building.

"People learned to swim like fish in the water, to fly like a bird in the sky, but on Earth, we still have to learn to live as brothers and sisters."

Quoting these words from Martin Luther King, the UNTAES Force Commander, Major-General Josef Scoops, underlined his commitment to bring peace to Eastern Slavonia, Baranja and Western Sirmium at a ceremony on March 14, marking the transfer of authority from the outgoing Sector Commander, Brigadier-General Freddy Van De Weghe. Along with Jacques, General Schoups reviewed the parade of troops from the Belgian, Russian, and Slovak Engineering Battalions at the airfield in Klisa. Belgian Defense Minister Jean-Pol Poncelot, who was accompanied by Chief of the Belgian Army Joint Staff, Admiral Willy Herteleer, represented the Belgian Government and its support and commitment to UNTAES. Slovak troops paraded at Klisa air base during which the President of the Serb Executive Council, Borislav Drzaic, the Head of the Croatian Government's Office of the Transitional Administration, Ivica Vrkic, Ambassadors from the United States, United Kingdom, France and Italy, and the Serb Commander General Dusan Loncar and Croat regional Commander General Djuro Decak joined UN officials at the ceremony. Calling it an important and historic occasion, Jacques said the Transfer of Authority parade participants "stood at the end of a terrible conflict that had divided family, neighbors and friends. He said he was confident that the beginning of a return to normalcy and reasoned dialogue was in sight". He stated "UNTAES would work to create the conditions to foster a sense of stability, thus paving the way for economic revitalization of the Region, reestablishing economic links, and reopening the borders to international trade and commerce."

180 Reunite at Family Meeting

A total of 180 people, 90 from each side, took part March 19th in the biggest family reunion held so far at the Sarvas-Nemetin crossing in the former zone of separation in Eastern Slavonia. Some of the people who attended the meeting, organized by ICRC and UNTAES Civil Affairs, had not seen each other for more than four years. People attended the meetings from both sides of the former confrontation line, often from mixed families, both Croat and Serb, or from minorities such as Hungarians or Slovaks whose relatives decided to remain in the Region at the start of the war.

ICRC spokesman Pat Fuller said he was optimistic that after demilitarization, those family meetings would be held inside the Region. "There were about 600 people on waiting lists to attend these meetings," said Fuller. The meetings of separated families were often very emotional.

At 7:30 AM on April 4th, 1996, a UN bus carrying 22 Serbs from llok, took the Sotin- Tovarnik-Delitovci-Nejemci-Podgradje-Lipovac route to Lipik and Pakrac. The Serbs were traveling to visit their houses in Western Slavonia under the safety and security assurances of UN-TAES and the Croatian Government. During the visit, the people dismounted from the buses, saw the places where they had lived, met with their friends and, in one case, a woman visited her son's grave. The Pakrac Police Chief met with the people and urged them to return to their homes. This was probably the most ambitious Village Visitation program so far. Earlier in March, three separate groups of the UNTAES village visitation program had given 22 displaced women from both sides of the former confrontation line the opportunity to see their neighborhoods and homes for the first time in five years.

"We are only going as far as the Bilje checkpoint, right?" asked a skeptical participant at the start of the first visit, organized on March 19, when seven Croatian women, displaced persons living in Osier, traveled through the villages of Bilje, Mace, Dada and Celiac in Baranja. The UNTAES motorcade passed through the checkpoint and into Baranja for a 90-minute visit that allowed the women to see their villages, their homes and, in one case, a family, after five years of separation.

What may have seemed unthinkable in the past became a reality as people crossed from both sides of the former confrontation line in the Region to visit Pakrac, Lipid, Osier, Serves and villages in Baranja.

<u>UNTAES views the village visitation</u>

Serbian women from Baranja traveled to Osier. My son discouraged me from coming. He said that anything like this would be dangerous.

But I told him that such a program was a necessary prelude to returning people to their villages. "It increases contacts, allowing people to know each other, allowing them to see their former homes and their former neighborhoods," said a Civil Affairs officer.

It could happen to us over there, that there could be demonstrations or incidents. But I told him to have confidence in the Mission of UNTAES because it is the only hope for peaceful reintegration of the Region of Eastern Slavonia, Baranja and Western Sirmium into the Republic of Croatia.

Grateful

As one Serb woman said, "I can say it felt very good. I want to thank everyone who made it possible for me to meet my parents after five years. I am very grateful...I am very excited. Everything changes with time, but my longing for Osier remains the same."

A senior Civil Affairs Officer, Graham Day, said "we intend to expand the scope and frequency of the program. People go into the region and they go out of the region and they see it's safe. I also think it's recognition of women in society. The women are not associated with the war activities that have ravaged this region. They are associated with more peaceful and more hopeful times in the future".

All four visits passed smoothly with no security problems. The UNTAES Civil Affairs Officer's served as the liaison between the two sides in arranging the date of the visits.

The Ukrainian Helicopter Squadron established its base at Klisa airfield and was already carrying out on average 16 sorties a day over the Region. Commanded by Ukrainian Air Force Colonel Serge Saticoy, the Helicopter Squadron was a self-contained unit and had more than 300 members including pilots, maintenance workers, radar station technicians, ground personnel and other specialists.

There were four MI-S helicopters and several MI-24 heavy-duty battle helicopters. Other MI-8's and equipment arrived in April. The main objective of their reconnaissance was to get acquainted with all the available helipads or sites on which their helicopters could land. They also were prepared for medical evacuations, and transportation of personnel, inside and outside of the Region.

Help Arrives for Grieving Mothers

The news was delivered to Milk Agric that her son had died that day. Someone asked her check with an UNTAES officer whether she could attend his funeral in Osier. On learning the details, the UN office swung into action. A civil affairs officer went to pick up Ms. Agric, her daughter and granddaughter at their village. They reached the cemetery at 5:00 pm, where several hundred family members, relative's neighbors and curious onlookers, both Serbs and Croats, had gathered. At the suggestion of the Croatian authorities, the family, represented by three generations, visited the dead man's family house and exchanged notes about life then and now. At 9:00 pm, the women returned to their homes sad at the loss but happy that they could lay the man to rest.

Joint Committees Develop Cooperation

Upon establishing UNTAES, U.N. Secretary-General Boutros Boutros-Ghali recommended the Transitional Administrator for the Region set up functional implementation committees in eight major areas on civilian and other administrative tasks. These Committees were the essential building blocks used to develop cooperation throughout the area and ensure a sense of security for the population.

The Civil Affairs component of the UNTAES mission organized a series of meetings with authorities on both sides soon after the Security Council note to establish the committees. It was always recognized that this might not be enough and that each of the eight main committees might need to have sub-committees. It was therefore meant to be a slowly expanding network of joint arrangements. The UNTAES Bulletin regularly reported to readers about accomplishments and developments as the work proceeded.

Implementation Committee on Public Services to restore normal functioning (including water, sanitation, energy supply, public transport, communications, waste disposal, health and educational facilities) and to oversee the rebuilding of houses damaged or destroyed during the conflict;

Implementation Committee on Civil Administration to identify how the administrative structures of the parties correspond with each other; to oversee local judicial procedures; to oversee matters relating to the transitional budgets, revenues and expenditures; and to oversee internal and external transport and communications links;

Implementation Committee on the Return of Refugees and Displaced Persons. UNHCR was the lead agency for such returns. Its tasks were to coordinate and control the voluntary return of refugees and displaced persons;

Implementation Committee on Police to establish a temporary police force, define its structure and size; develop a training program and oversee its implementation.

Implementation Committee on Human Rights to establish the human rights monitoring mission; establish liaison with Council of Europe human rights bodies (European Commission and Court on Human Rights), monitor and report on human rights violations.

Implementation Committee on Education and Culture to establish procedures and regulations to help ethnic minorities.

Implementation Committee on Records was designed to develop appropriate records for individuals living in the new area.

Demilitarization Begins

One of the most important objectives of the UNTAES' mission was to ensure the full and complete demilitarization of the region, as a stepping-stone to peace, security and economic development. I believe we made progress towards our goals and encouraged the people of the region to look at and listen to what we were doing to secure a better and more stable life for all. Weapons had to be eliminated and bunkers removed from the area. UNTAES military and police forces were available to ensure security. General Schoup's reported he was ready for his mission. We wanted people to know about our plans so we could cooperate in the most important step…a safer and more secure future for the Region.

The basic agreement of November 12, 1995 explained that the "the region would be demilitarized according to the schedule and procedures determined by the international force". The UNTAES military force had arrived in the region and training of a joint police force had begun.

We wanted people to know about the processes we established and that we would ensure the personal security of families. We wanted everyone to know who would be authorized to retain weapons, how police authority would work and how heavy weapons would be destroyed.

What was meant by demilitarization?

Demilitarization meant that military equipment and weapons would be either removed from the region or collected and destroyed. All barracks and related facilities were to be handed over to the transitional administration, which decided how to destroy them. Demilitarization also meant the disbanding and demobilization of all military forces, except for a police force, which was kept in place to maintain law and order. As demilitarization was carried out, personnel returned to civilian life. Demobilized soldiers could wear their uniforms but without insignia or rank. Military forces included all regular, paramilitary, irregular, volunteer units and armed groups present in the region. Police forces included all regular, special, border and all other units referred to as militia.

How demilitarization occurred

On April 15, 1996 Jacques, signed the plan for the demilitarization of the UNTAES region. This document had been transmitted to local civilian, military and police authorities of the region. To carry out the plan, we established procedures emphasizing the cooperation of local military and police commanders. Local commanders organized the disbanding of units, the collection of military weapons and equipment and transfer of infrastructures. UNTAES forces set up a number *of* weapons collection points, which were under their exclusive control. Upon receipt, weapons were destroyed.

For the local civilian population, demilitarization meant no one was allowed to carry or transport any weapon—unless specifically authorized by UNTAES. Police allowed civilian weapons to be retained in accordance with the law and would issue permits. Previous weapons authorizations were invalid regardless of the originating authority. According to the law, those who retained any authorized weapons at home had to register them through local police. A procedure for registering weapons was announced. Unauthorized weapons, ammunition, explosives and military equipment was handed over to UNTAES patrols or to the closest UNTAES compound. This had to be done before the end of the demilitarization period. The objective of the demilitarization was very clear...to reestablish a peaceful environment and return to normal civilian life.

When did demilitarization happen?

The official notification for the start of the demilitarization process was announced by UNTAES and police authorities and broadcast on TV and radio stations. The process started before the end of May and was completed within 30 days. Subsequently, no one in the region was allowed to carry or transport weapons in public without special authorization. Anyone carrying weapons after demilitarization was completed was in violation of the regulations. The militia, who was assisted by UNTAES forces, maintained strict control. Anyone violating the weapons ban was subject to arrest and to be judged in the local courts.

All borders were under the supervision and monitoring of UNTAES in order to prohibit, by force if necessary, any weapons from entering the region.

What about security?

Security in the region was already ensured by our forces, which were now fully deployed. The force consisted of 5,000 troops. The mission of the force was twofold: to maintain security in the region by preventing armed infiltration and to assist the demilitarization process. The militia maintained order and enforced laws, working in close cooperation with UNTAES authorities. By this time, everything was in place to start demilitarization...The Transitional Administration, the UNTAES military force and the Militia.

CHAPTER 6

UNTAES IN PICTURES

UNTAES had many roles in the region. Here we show some of the activities that took place.

The healing power of religion

The Catholic and Orthodox Easter services were held in the churches in Ilok and Dalj on April 7th and 14th respectively. Both services attracted large gatherings and were peaceful. The local militia handled security in a calm and professional manner.

Dalj

UNTAES Transitional Administrator Jacques Klein believed that religion played an important role in creating conditions for the healing process to take root. In his meetings with religious leaders, he expressed his hope that they would take a more ecumenical and reconciliatory position and develop links between the Orthodox and Catholic believers. We visited at least one church each Sunday when Jacques was in the region.

Family reunion meetings in Bilje and Nustar

Jacques (right) meets in Erdut with the international community's high representative for Bosnia and Herzegovina, Carl Bildt.

Opening of UNTAES Headquarters in Vukovar

The new Czech field surgical hospital was officially opened at Klisa on April 22, 1996. Speaking at the inauguration, UNTAES force commander, Major General Joseph Shoups said; "this hospital will provide the specialized medical care that is not available at the battalion level. Minor surgical help can be done at battalion medical centers but major interventions will be done in this hospital."

Dr. Mojmir Mrva, the chief-surgeon led a team of more than 40 personnel, which included an orthopedist, neurosurgeon, an anesthetist, ear, nose and throat specialist and a dentist.

On the question of community welfare, Dr. Mrva said, "Although our tasks are restricted to UN personnel, in emergency cases we are ready to help every patient in the area."

The hospital is well equipped with modem facilities for intensive care. A clinical laboratory can carry out blood tests, urine analysis or hematological testing. There is an ultrasound machine that can be used for investigating liver or kidney ailments, a mobile x-ray machine with a thermo printer and TV monitor. Another operates a machine for examination of blood samples, including the radiometric testing of blood gas levels.

Czech Field Surgical Hospital

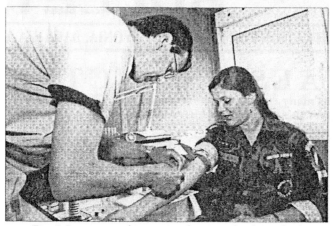

Dr. Mrva examines a patient at the hospital

The hospital is a continuation of the Czech field surgical team that worked initially in the former sector South in Knin. In December 1995, it replaced the American mash unit in Pleso, Zagreb before being relocated to Klisa.

There are three wards for male and female patients, including a ward for patients with infectious diseases. The hospital could accommodate and treat 20 in-bed patients at a time. The number of outpatients that could be diagnosed was unlimited. The Czech surgical team maintained close cooperation and coordination with the Ukrainian rescue helicopter service, particularly with regard to the speedy transfer of accident victims in the field.

Family reunions held for first time in Bilje and Nustar

A new landmark in the organizing of family reunions was reached when separated families from inside and outside the region met for the first time in Bilje and Nustar on April 24 and 26. Until then, family reunions were held within the former zone of separation between Sarvas and Nemetin.

In Bilje, 41 people from the Baranja met with 49 people from outside the region.

In Nustar, 107 people from Mirkovci met with 86 family members from outside the region.

Following the confidence generated by these reunions, representatives of the Red Cross from both sides decided upon the following schedule for reunions:

Tuesdays at the Sarvas-Nemetin crossing with 35 people from each side;

Thursdays at the Nustar crossing with 70 people from each side;

Fridays at the Bilje crossing with 50 people from each side.

Family reunions organized by the local and international Red Cross and UNTAES enabled more than 2,000 people separated by the conflict to meet each other.

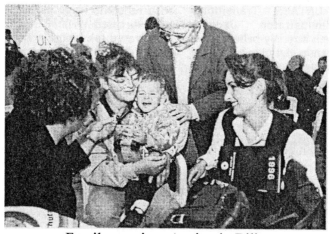

Family reunion meeting in Bilje

Several hundred people had registered at their local Red Cross offices to meet with their family members from the other side of the former confrontation lines. "We want to give as many people as possible the chance to see each other at these meetings", says Zeljko Cengija from the Beli Manastir Red Cross. "Priority went to immediate family members, but once we exhausted the lists, we opened it up to include friends and relatives", he said.

A donation of six Rub hall tents by the international federation of the Red Cross contributed to creating a more spacious environment for meetings, as they were able to accommodate up to 200 people at a time. "Sometimes we had to limit participation to one family member from each side because of the tremendous interest," said Stephan Ham of the Osijck Red Cross. "The tents meant that entire families could take part and sit with some degree of comfort during the two-hour visit periods."

Zagreb-Belgrade Highway Reopens to International Traffic

Customs Officers inspect a car

The E-70 motorway between Zagreb and Belgrade reopened to international traffic on Tuesday May 7, 1996 after almost five years. The motorway had been sealed off in a seven-kilometer stretch following the war in 1991. "It was a major step forward", said Klein, after cutting the ribbon at a formal ceremony in the presence of the traffic and communications minister of the Federal Republic of Yugoslavia, Zoran Vujovic, the Croatian deputy prime minister, Ivica Kostovic and other top officials from both sides. "Its one of the many steps we have already undertaken in the process of normalization."

UNTAES patrolled parts of the highway that ran through the region. "Roads are the arteries of nations for people, trade and commerce. They bring countries together", said Jacques.

On the same day, the UNTAES deputy transitional administrator, Derek Boothby, inaugurated the reopening of the Adriatic oil pipeline, shut down for the past five years. The Croatian pipeline manager Ante Cicinsain and the Pancevo refinery manager Radovan Pesikan were present at the occasion.

Mosquito spraying of the Region

Due to security concerns, aerial spraying for mosquitoes was not carried out during a four-year period in Osijek, causing alarming health and Environment problems. Therefore, it was one of the first issues to be raised when the joint implementation committee meetings started. It was accepted that mosquitoes made no distinction between Serbs and Croats or anyone else and the menace had to be fought jointly. Agreement was reached on the various operational and financial aspects. Experts from both sides carried out tests in the region. At 6:00 A.M. on Sunday, May 19, the spraying began. Initially covering the Baranja and the city of Osijek, the exercise extended over the rest of the UNTAES region. By Wednesday May 22nd, the operation was concluded. Five Croatian planes carrying special UN markings made a total of 14 flights. Croat pilots flew the planes with Serb co-pilots. Two UN attack helicopters provided safety and emergency support while a third helicopter with the mosquito experts on board monitored the operation. Flights covered an area of 22,000 hectares and the cost of the project was estimated at over $200,000 dollars.

Jacques exchanges first mailbags with Mr. Vrkic and Mr. Hadzic.

First mail exchange

On Friday, May 10, Serb and Croatian delegations met between the UNTAES checkpoint at the Nustar and Bras Din crossings and conducted the first exchange of mail between the UNTAES region and other parts of Croatia. The UNTAES administrator lifted the first two mailbags and made a symbolic exchange of the mailbags with Ivica Vrkic, head of the Croatian government's office for UNTAES and Goran Hadzic, head of the local Serb authorities. Commenting on the importance of the event, Klein said, "This again opens the region more, and allows people to communicate...which is our goal. The goal is to bring people back together and mail is a key element in that process."

The renewal of postal service was arranged through the work of a joint implementation committee chaired by UNTAES civil affairs with Serb and Croat delegations.

In order for someone in the UNTAES region to mail a letter, all that person had to do was to go to the local post office and pay for postage, as usual. However, a stamp was not necessary because the letter or parcel was directed to the main post office (Vukovar in the south, Beli Manastir in the Baranja) and there it was marked with a special stamp saying "UNTAES: postage paid" in both English and French. The post was then directed to the transit post office at the Nustar or Bilje crossing. Exchanges of mail took place on Tuesdays, Thursdays and Saturdays at 8:00 A.M. Representatives of HPT and PTT waited at each side of the crossing in their vehicles and were escorted to the place where the mail-scanning device was located. Personnel of HPT scanned their own post under the surveillance of a PTT member and vice versa. After scanning, both sides were escorted back to their respective areas with the bags of mail.

This arrangement was a temporary one and was the first step towards fully integrating the postal services.

Citizens clean up Vukovar bus station

Women of all ages hard at work

Various women's groups in the region organized a three-day project of clearing and beautifying the town bus station. UNTAES Slovak engineers provided equipment to level the place and clean the debris. More than 50 trucks of soil were spread to fill the beds where flowers and trees were planted.

Questions and Answers

Question: Currently, all men of military age here think that the Croatians want to try them as war criminals. Is this true?

Answer - No. The Croatian government has recently adopted a new law on amnesty for those involved in the fighting over the past five years, except for people charged with "war crimes" and certain other criminal acts. The transitional administrator strongly believes in the need for a clear and unequivocal amnesty and has supported that idea in discussions with all high-ranking Croatian government officials. We believe that the amnesty bill needed to be specific about amnesty except for "war crimes" as defined by international law. This meant that the great majority of individuals would be covered by amnesty.

The administrator is continuing his efforts to achieve an unambiguous amnesty law.

Question -UN cars and trucks speed through our village and make it dangerous to walk on the roads. Why don't they slow down? And why don't they ever stop for people who want to ride with them for a short distance?

Answer: We agree with your concern and we apologize. Nobody should drive too fast. Transitional Administrator Klein has recently issued the strictest orders that all UN military and civilian personnel must obey local speed laws. UN military police have been instructed to take firm action to stop speeding cars anywhere in the region. We hope this will improve the situation immediately.

We regret that UN regulations forbid any UN employee from picking up casual passengers. Problems of communication, misunderstandings, safety, insurance and legal considerations are some of the reasons for this policy.

CHAPTER 7

COMMUNICATION-THE KEY TO SUCCESS

Opening up communications in the Region was a big deal. One of the facts that we touted was that "more than 20,000 phone calls were made to people inside the Zone of Separation on the first day that phones were reconnected. Privately, we joked that about 19, 000 of those calls were death threats to those people still living inside the Zone of Separation.

<u>Telephone Links Restored Between Beli Manastir and Osijek</u>

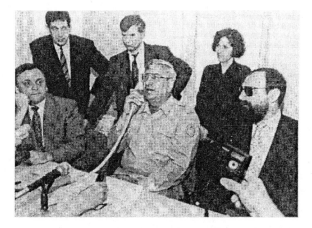

Jacques made the first operational phone call to open up the Region. Also present were Mr. Vrkic and Mr. Hadzic. Telephone links between

73

the Baranja region and the rest of Croatia were reestablished on Tuesday, May 21, as part of an agreement reached by the UNTAES Joint Implementation Committee (JIC) on Public Utilities.

Jacques hosted the official ceremony in the Beli Manastir Post Office to mark this event. In attendance were a Croatian delegation led by Mr. Ivica Vrkic and a delegation of local Serb authorities led by Mr. Goran Hadzic.

"This is another step in bringing people together. Whether it's the highway, the railroad, which we hope to open soon, the mail, which we have already done, and now the telephone system. There is only one goal- that is to bring people together and that is what we are going to do here today," said Klein, before placing the first phone call on the newly installed telecommunications system to the UN Liaison Office in Zagreb.

The equipment provided by Croatian Post and Telecommunications (HPT") allowed for 15 outgoing and 15 incoming lines at a time between Baranja and the rest of Croatia. For residents of Baranja, it did not affect or change telephone users' access to the Yugoslav communications system. They could still phone direct locally or internationally using the Yugoslav system.

However, it was then possible to phone the other areas of Croatia without using an international access code. In order to make a call to Osijek, for example, a person in Baranja needed first to dial zero, then the city code (031) and then the telephone number. This made calls to other Croatian regions four times cheaper.

According to the Beli Manastir Post Office, the lines were in constant use and the system worked as expected since being installed. The only problem was the very high load on the system because of the huge demand. The number of lines had to be increased.

The JIC on Public Utilities also worked out modalities that restored telephone connections between Vinkovci, Vukovar and Osijek by mid-June.

Handicraft items on display at the Borovo Bazaar

More than 60 delegates representing 40 international non-governmental organizations (NGOs) met at the Hotel Dunav in Vukovar on May 23rd. Klein, while addressing the gathering said, "The key task for all of us after demilitarization is to bring this area back to the economic status it once had. This area had one of the highest per capita standards of living in the former Yugoslavia. It was a rich area, now devastated by five years of conflict. The goal is now to put people back to work and to recreate an economy."

The Head of Civil Affairs, Dr. Gerard Fischer, said the international community had earmarked millions of US dollars to go towards various projects and requested that NGOs work with UNTAES to identify the needs of the Region. He also mentioned plans for a micro-loan program funded by the United States Agency for International Development (USAID) in which interest-free loans of $500 to $25,000 US dollars was provided to assist small businesses.

Two cases of cease-fire violations were reported southwest of Orolik on the nights of May 23 and 26, when UNTAES personnel were fired on from inside the former Zone of Separation. The source of fire could not be positively identified. In accordance with the rules of engagement, fire was returned on both occasions. No UN personnel were injured in the incidents. These incidents occurred periodically but never really got out of hand. The only real violence that we were aware of was the Belgian soldiers getting drunk and fighting on the weekends. One weekend, one soldier killed another soldier with a bayonet. It was just one of the things that the mission seemed to take in stride. A pilot project of registering pensioners eligible for payment by the Croatian Government began in the Baranja on May 28, when over two days some 188 persons registered for pensions with Croatian pension officials.

Several Women's Groups in the Region led by the Borovo Women's Group organized a "Charily Bazaar" at the Borovo Local Community Centre on May 31st to raise funds for several community welfare projects. Performing artists from Bobota and the Baranja presented folklore items to a packed and appreciative audience, which included more than 100, UNTAES staff members. Various stalls were set up to sell handicraft pieces, souvenirs and other items. The fortune teller had a large number of clients but the high- light of the evening was the buffet which was, enjoyed by all. When asked by the Civil Affairs Officer associated with the project if the event had generated enough money, one of the organizers said "That's not so important. We planned this event on our own, organized everything ourselves and made it happen successfully. That's more important. I have never seen our women so genuinely happy". A refugee woman from Petrovci left her vegetable and flower stall and danced to every song played. During an interlude, she whispered shyly to the Civil Affairs officer that she had been to a hair- dresser that morning for the first time in five years.

The Pakistani Battalion, which was one of the four Battalions deployed as part of the UNTAES Military component (the others being Belgian, Russian and Jordanian), officially took over its area of responsibility (AOR) in the Baranja on May 6.

The major element of PAKBAT, which had its headquarters in the Oarda castle, was a mechanized infantry Battalion, backed by a 14-tank armor squadron and a 6-gun artillery battery. A 20-bed field hospital with an operating room also formed part of the Battalion's assets to deal with medical emergencies.

Commanded by Colonel Tariq Rasool, the nearly 900 soldiers had a one-year deployment and were all well trained and equipped to carry out their mission. As the senior liaison officer, Major Faheem, said, "We are ready to carry out our tasks to facilitate the demilitarization of our Area of Responsibility (AOR), to monitor the safe return of displaced persons, to contribute by our presence to the maintenance of peace and security and to assist in the implementation of the Basic Agreement."

The PAKBAT was conducting frequent social patrols on foot to establish contact with the population and familiarize themselves with the territory. In sharing with the Belgians the responsibility for covering the Baranja, the Pakistanis have been able to increase the frequency and number of foot patrols and the monitoring and manning of crossing points and observation posts.

Face-to-Face Contact with People

Local Mayors and other authorities organized the town hall meetings. Senior officers from UNTAES Civil Affairs, Public Affairs, UN Military Observers (UNMOS) and UN Civilian Police (CIVPOL) talked to the people and took their questions. The Mayor of Tenja, Mr. Pavle Stojankovic said these meetings were necessary for people to understand UNTAES and its mandate. While addressing a town hall meeting in Tenja, Gerard Fischer, the Head of Civil Affairs said that the overall message to the people was to remain here and work together on the issue of peaceful reintegration. "We have to introduce the concept of living together, of coexisting together, of reconciliation. We can only plant the seeds for that. On the Croat side there must be understanding that many people who have been caught in the war have not been necessarily part of the war. They are part of the Region; they have a right

77

to be here. They have to have the same privileges and obligations as any Croat citizen."

Town hall meetings were held in Ludvinci, Sarengrad, Tompojevci, Bobota, Tenja, Brsadin, Vcra, Berak, Miklusevic, Boksic, and Mirkovci and in the Baranja. The UNTAES office in Ilok organized a public information program for the population. Representatives from Civil Affairs, UNMOs and CIVPOL were present to answer questions raised. Meetings were held between 10:00 A.M. and noon every Monday, Wednesday and Friday at the Mayor's office in Ilok. In Tovarnik, meetings were conducted on Thursdays between 1830 and 2000 hours at the Mayor's office. In Bapska, it was between 4:00 P.M. and 6:00 P.M.

UNTAES Civil Affairs facilitated the participation of 12 farmers (eight women and four men) from the Vukovar and Dalj municipalities for a Seminar on Organic Farming held at the Agricultural Faculty in Darda. Six farmers from the Baranja region also attended.

CHAPTER 8

TRANSITIONAL POLICE FORCE DEPLOYS

Putting together the Transitional Police Force (TPF) was a real trick because the Serbs and Croats still hated each other. It's no wonder, since they had been fighting each other for years. Getting the first two policemen together at the Russian checkpoint between Vukovar and Osijek and then getting them to take a photograph…and smile…was a real highlight. While things were rocky for a while, having the Swedish and Irish police running the show for the Mission was a touch of genius. We had to be very careful not to Americanize the Mission too much because not only would we antagonize the Serbs, we had a tendency to antagonize the UN leadership.

Following the demilitarization of the Region, the role of insuring Law and Order in the UNTAES area of responsibility was taken over by the Transitional Police Force (TPF). Preparations for the deployment of the TPF began early in March 1995 when lists were drawn by the Serb and Croatian sides to enroll their professional policemen in special courses sponsored by the International Criminal Investigative Training Assistance Program (ICITAP) of the United States Department of Justice.

All policemen from each side had their names submitted to and approved by the other side through UNTAES organized meetings of the

Joint Implementation Committee on Police Matters. UN Civilian Police Commissioner Haakon Jurors of Sweden headed this effort. The two-week-long special training began in Budapest in March and by the end of June had trained 288 Serb and Croatian policemen.

At the same time UN CIVPOL began to co-locate with local Militia in the 11 stations of the Region…eight in the southern part and three in Baranja.

TRANSITIONAL
POLICE FORCE
THE REGION OF EASTERN SLAVONIA
BARANJA AND WESTERN SIRMIUM

Hgt: 185 cm

Eye col: BLUE Dob: 6/18/63

EXPIRES

15

JUN

97

No: TPF 1317
Wpn: 69502

The TPF Special ID card

There were approximately 350 CIVPOL monitors from over 20 countries manning the stations 16-hours a day. The main task was to see that local police performed their duties in accordance with existing international standards and ensure there were no violations of fundamental human rights.

Demilitarization Completed

On Friday June 21, the Joint Implementation Committee (JIC) for Military Affairs met for the last time following the successful completion of demilitarization of the UNTAES Region. The Administrator and Force Commander met with the Serb Military Commander, General Loncar, and the Commander of the Osijek Operation Zone, General Decak at the Sarvas-Nemetin crossing to signal the end of the military phase of demilitarization covering the removal of tanks, artillery, multiple rocket launchers and other heavy weapons. Klein complimented the professionalism of the Serb and Croatian Generals and said that one of the reasons for the exercise passing without incident was that the two Generals had lived up to their agreement.

Force Commander General Schoups with General Loncar and General Decak in an earlier meeting

At the conclusion of the second phase of inspecting barracks and installations, General Schoups signed the final demilitarization order. The TPF was to be issued a different uniform with a common Identification Card, and ultimately be comprised of 1,300 officers. Initially the size was somewhat smaller. They functioned under the control of the Transitional Administrator and the Croatian Government paid their salaries.

Courses were conducted in Erdut to train 600 Serbs employed by the Militia and later they were eligible for induction into the TPF. The Erdut course was a shortened version of the Budapest program, running six days rather than 10 and training only Serbs rather than a combined class of Croats and Serbs.

The first week in Erdut started with 130 Serbs split into classes taught by American instructors, all of whom had law enforcement and instructional backgrounds. The training ended on June 22.

Steve Hargrove, the ICITAP director of training, explained that ICI-TAP had worked in many countries with a similar program of training police officers, but that aspects of the course were adapted in particular to the conditions of the conflict here. Hargrove emphasized the fact that all of the police officers attending the TPF courses were professionals and already familiar with many of the subjects and techniques discussed.

The ethnic composition of the region was to be reflected in the ethnic makeup of the members of the TPF itself. CIVPOL played a monitoring role in the administration of the TPF in conformity with international standards.

Mr. Hargrove explained the transition: "It's not as if a whole group of strange people are going to show up one day. It's not going to be a drastic change other than the uniform, which is a drastic change for people".

"The fact is that it's the same people with new ideas, and with some new direction in the areas of police service. Hopefully the new look will ensure impartial safety and security for all the residents of the Region." The Transitional Police will have the primary responsibility for maintaining law and order in the Region.

After months of de-mining and other repair work, the first test run of the railway track between Vinkovci and Tovarnik was carried out on Thursday June 27. A crowd watched excitedly as the engine with Klein on board rolled out of Vinkovci station pulling along a train carrying other Government and railroad officials. This was the first time in five years that a train moved in the easterly direction. The reopening of the Sid-Vinkovci rail line depended on the normalization of relations between the Federal Republic of Yugoslavia and Croatia.

Jacques completes first successful train ride in the area

"The Music Bridge", a cultural program of dance and music sponsored by the Force Commander, General Schoups, was held at the Serb Cultural Center of Vukovar on June 27th. Conceived by Monique Ponte, a Belgian military staff member and Zivka Komlenac, a poetess from Vukovar, the event brought together artists from the Region and from within UNTAES. An art exhibition was the other highlight of the evening.

Major Alex Karelin of the Russian Army displays his guitar playing abilities

A spectacular ground and air show was organized by UNTAES at the Borovo Aero club airfield on Wednesday June 26th. Dedicated to the children of the Region, it was an evening of music, dance, fun and excitement. Some very young talent provided live entertainment from Vukovar and Borovo. Russian Federation Paratroopers displayed their parachuting skills and Ukrainian Helicopters carried out low-flying maneuvers. All children had the opportunity to ride on UNTAES combat vehicles. Klein, Boothby, General Schoups and hundreds of UN-TAES military and civilian personnel participated in the event.

Picture perfect landing

Getting a closer look

Free Legal Aid Available

Mr. Eide (left) and Mr. Galbraith officially open the Vukovar office

The Civil Rights Project aimed to provide free, legal assistance to residents of the UNTAES region and officially got underway on July 9 with ribbon-cutting ceremonies held in its offices in Osijek and Vukovar.

Jacques Klein, United States Ambassador-At-Large, U.S. Ambassador to Croatia, Peter Galbraith and Norwegian diplomat Kai Eide attended the Vukovar opening of the project, funded by Norway and the United States.

Jacques stressed the importance of this kind of international support in the success of the UNTAES mandate: "We cannot change the past but we can try to shape the future. On behalf of the United Nations, I want to thank the Kingdom of Norway, the Government of the United States and their representatives here for turning words into deeds and helping us turn swords into ploughshares".

The Civil Rights Project emerged out of the joint efforts of the United States Agency for International Development and the Norwegian Refugee Council offices in Osijek and Beli Manastir.

Vukovar provided legal assistance to persons residing in and returning to the areas of Eastern Slavonia, Baranja and Western Sirmium. The project assisted people in the protection of their human and civil rights by providing access to and explanations of the legal and administrative system of Croatia.

Mr. Galbraith remarked that the protection of individual rights is the foundation of the Basic Agreement, saying the key to its success is the protection "of the right of the people who live in this area to become full citizens of Croatia with exactly the same equal rights as everybody else, and not the slightest discrimination against such people was tolerable.

The project director Ole Rasmussen said the offices would start operating "once staffing was completed".

He anticipated that most queries would center on the issues of citizenship law, property rights, financial obligations and family law.

Commercial Traffic set to use Drava

In yet another important step towards the reestablishment of communication links between the Region and the rest of the Republic of Croatia, Jacques symbolically opened the Drava River on July 9th to economic traffic. Joined by representatives of the Croatian and local Serb sides, he was on board one of a flotilla of four boats which traveled the 23 km from the confluence of the Danube and Drava Rivers to Osijek.

The opening of the Drava River and the beginning of work to restore the port of Vukovar are parallel projects of UNTAES, expected to greatly benefit the region economically. Jacques explained: "We know that one job in a harbor converts to ten jobs in the hinterland. Now with Osijek open to the Danube, we are looking forward to the rebuilding of Vukovar and to have complementary ports here that profit a nation as a whole."

The UNTAES Joint Implementation Committee on Military Affairs provided the forum for initial discussions on how to prepare the Drava River for the resumption of commercial traffic. The first step in this process was the de-mining of the river itself. Both Croatian and local Serb units began the de-mining on June 24th and completed it ten days later. Now that UNTAES and the two parties agree that the river is fully de-mined, a survey is to be conducted to determine whether dredging the Drava will be necessary after the five-year absence of traffic.

However, residents of the area are cautioned that the de-mining of the riverbank and the portion of the river northwest of Osijek is continuing. Therefore, people should not go near the river unless they know that a particular area has been declared safe.

Pensions paid in Darda

A total of 150 pensions were paid to people in Darda on July 10th following the successful completion of the UNTAES pilot pension project. Head of Civil Affairs, Gerard Fischer, attended the start of the payment procedure. "We are here today to start with a scheme worked out with the Croatian Government. We will start paying pensions to people who have earned their money through work and contributions to the Croatian pension fund. This is the outcome of the pilot project which was limited to the area of Darda and contains a total of 175 pensioners, most of whom will today obtain their first pension," said Mr. Fischer as officials from the Croatian Government's pension fund began the first payments.

Darda, in Baranja, was selected as the location of the pilot project at the end of May, when 175 people registered. Processing applications by the Croatian pension fund led to 150 people meeting the requirements to receive a pension immediately.

Payments were made in Kuna with the average pension issued being the equivalent of 200 Deutsch marks.

The Joint Implementation Committee on Civil Administration is working out the modalities to open administrative offices in the UNTAES region to address issues such as pension registration.

Start of the payment pension process in Darda

The arrival of Belgian peacekeepers to Baranja in April 1992 marked the start of the United Nations presence in the Region. Since that date, Belgian Battalions have completed rotations in Baranja. The current battalion, BELBAT XII, began its four-month tour of duty at the beginning of April.

More than half of the 616 troops making up BELBAT XII have served in Baranja before. The Belbat commander, Lieutenant-Colonel Alain Reynaert, also served in Sector East Headquarters in 1993.

The Belgian Battalion HQ in Beli Manastir and three companies were deployed in the northern half of Baranja. Belgian peacekeepers were stationed at several border posts along the Drava. With the end of demilitarization, BELBAT troops also manned a checkpoint at the Bettina Bridge monitoring all incoming and outgoing vehicles for weapons.

BELBAT XII carried on the practice established by its predecessors of high visibility and contact with the local population. One of the most important forms of this was through the medical assistance provided by BELBAT doctors. They were sometimes the only source of medical care available to people, especially those in remote villages.

While we touted the great progress made by troops leading the demining efforts, we did suffer some losses. I remember stories about individual soldiers, both men and women, sustaining terrible wounds due to land mines. In one day I remember that one soldier lost an arm, another part of his leg and that one female soldier had lost an eye. So, this de-mining effort was not without loss. These efforts were always difficult.

De-mining starts in Lipovach

Workers begin de-mining in Lipovac

De-mining began in Lipovac, one of several villages on UNTAES territory selected for a resettlement pilot project. Klein traveled to Lipovac on July 10th to announce the official start of de-mining. He took the opportunity to emphasize the high priority, which UNTAES had giving to the return of all displaced persons. Croatian de-mining specialists worked in cooperation with UNTAES; however, the area remained under UNTAES supervision.

CHAPTER 9

THE DJELETOVCI OIL FIELDS

The Djeletovci oil fields were of critical importance because they were the financial life's-blood of the Region. The sooner we were able to get the oil fields up and running and producing products and money for the people of the Region, the better off they all would be. There was great anticipation the day we held the press conference to re-open the oil fields. Jacques was to make the announcement but for some last minute reason, could not make the event. We pressed on without him, making the announcement, and everyone involved seemed pleased. The press liked it and the participants congratulated each other on a job very well done indeed.

Agreement was reached on July 25th that led to a return of production at the Djeletovci oil fields. It was agreed that a joint team of Croatian, Serb and UNTAES experts would start a survey on the condition of the fields. UNTAES Civil Affairs chief, Gerard Fischer said there were intense negotiations between both sides on a number of issues. The 10-day assessment mission began on July 26. On August 6, the first phase of de-mining of the Djeletovci oil fields began. This and all other activities were done between a local de-mining company and Croatian experts.

Oil exploitation began on August 15. Although all fields were not tapped immediately, oil production started in those areas declared clear by the de-mining team.

Djeletovci Oil Field

On the issue of Serb employees of the former Naftna Industrial Krajina (NIK) retaining their jobs under the Croatian company Industrial Nafta (INA), there was broad agreement to rehire them, within the structures of INA, in a phased manner. Not all people had jobs immediately, but INA found other locations for them to be absorbed. As Fischer said "INA is a huge company and there shouldn't be a problem rehiring Serbs, if there is a political will to carry it out."

Over 150 former NIK employees were given draft contracts to be re-hired. A further meeting with a larger number of former employees was scheduled for August.

Another step in opening the Region to the rest of Croatia was taken on August 25th when Jacques inaugurated the opening of the road between Vukovar and Osijek via Klisa, in the presence of Croatian and local Serb authorities.

The Vukovar to Osijek road

Following an agreement between the U.N., NATO and IFOR, the first exercise of NATO-IFOR aircraft flying over the UNTAES Region was carried out on July 25th. IFOR and NATO aircraft were available to support the UNTAES mission and to support the security of the Region. In order to properly plan for any eventuality, there were regular exercises in the air, generally at very high altitudes but occasionally in sight of people on the ground. This was especially interesting to those of us on the ground that would have enjoyed seeing a U.S. Air Force or Navy jet streaking across the skies but apparently there was too much concern at very high levels about being shot down by the bad guys. And that would have caused everybody a problem.

In view of the acute shortage of fuel in the Region, UNTAES arranged to procure 300 liters of fuel for use in maintaining essential services. This buffer stock helped facilitate continued patrolling by Transitional Police Force (TPF) vehicles. As an emergency measure, 5,000 liters of petrol and 5,000 liters of diesel were also supplied to the Vukovar hospital on July 25th. We had found earlier that the Russian troops had "appropriated" the UN oil and was selling it on the open market to the locals. Problem was that their own government wasn't paying them, so they had to survive any way they could. I'm told we looked the other way on this issue.

A wine competition in cooperation with local wine growers was organized on July 26th in the predominantly ethnic Hungarian village of

Zmajevac. This annual event was held for the first time since 1991. More than 50 wine growers representing the villages of Zmajevac, Suza, Draz, Karanac, Knezevi Vinogradi and Kotlina took part in the competition. A jury pre-selected the wines and awarded prizes. Derek Boothby, Deputy Transitional Administrator, headed the UNTAES delegation at the event.

On July 28, twelve children from an ethnically mixed group of Serbs, Croats and Ruthenians belonging to the village of Petrovci, left the Region for a two-and-a-half week holiday in Austria. UNTAES Civil Affairs organized the travel documents required to cross from the Region, Croatia, Hungary and Austria. The holiday was offered courtesy of the Austrian Embassy in Zagreb and a Non-Governmental Organization (NGO)...Red Falcon-Dorbiach.

Border Monitoring has an Impact on Traffic

As a convoy of trucks loaded with timber pulled up at the border crossing point in Bapska, regional authorities routinely stopped the trucks and asked for documents. Realizing they had none, the authorities promptly detained the trucks for illegally taking timber out of the Region. "This", says Alistair Livingston, Chief of the UNTAES Border Monitors, "has been one of the most significant impacts of our presence at the international borders between the Federal Republic of Yugoslavia (FRY), Hungary, and the Region."

Border Monitors at the Erdut Bridge

UNTAES Border Monitors began deploying across the nine crossing points in May establishing two regional headquarters, one in Ilok covering the south and the other in Beli Manastir covering the north. The initial group from Germany, France, America, Sweden, Finland, Great Britain and Russia, were former monitors for the International Conference of the Former Yugoslavia (ICFY) operating in FRY along the border with Bosnia during the sanctions. Hence they brought their special skills and breadth of experience to the job in the UNTAES Region.

Monitoring a car inspection

Border Monitors worked in close cooperation and coordination with the Transitional border police and customs, and with the UNTAES Military. Incoming vehicles were checked for arms and ammunition by UNTAES military elements, concurrently with international border controls carried out by transitional authorities. Departing vehicles were checked for compliance with export regulations in order to ensure that illegal transfer of items from the Region was denied. Such items as dismantled factory or farm machinery and high-value timber, came in for particular scrutiny. UNTAES looked for proper export documentation and allowed legitimate cross-border business and travel to continue, while working to stop illegal exports.

Maintaining a 24-hour presence at Ilok, Tovarnik, Batina and Erdut, the Border Monitors were an effective deterrent to illegal activity. Along with the UNTAES military presence a 'cordon sanitaire' was built at the crossings. They also contributed greatly to building confidence among the local people who saw that the law of the land was being properly implemented equally for all people. During the transitional period, we facilitated the substitution of the existing border and customs regime with the regime of the Republic of Croatia.

Indonesian Medical Company (Indomedcoy)

The Indomedcoy joined UNTAES on March 15, 1996, replacing its former national medical unit called Indomedbat. Its 72- strong contingent included 17-specialist doctors, besides other qualified personnel like communication experts and engineers. The Commander, Major Obedient, M.D., said "his unit believed strongly in the Hippocratic Oath and never refused medical assistance to anybody who entered their compound in Erdut." In the period between the set up of their medical facilities in Saponia, Erdut, in March and until the end of June, Indomedcoy provided primary and advanced medical care to more than 1,000 local people.

Delivering WHO medical supplies in Tenja

Since they received many patients with respiratory problems, doctors carried out a survey to find out the main causes, so they could suggest remedial measures. Although they managed with supplies brought from Indonesia, the World Heath Organization (WHO), Indomedcoy and WHO also coordinated on distribution of medical supplies to other local medical centers. Out of the six ambulances at their disposal, four vehicles were fully armored for use in emergency evacuations. In order to cover any eventuality, Indomedcoy ambulances were always deployed at family reunion meetings, village visitations and at demining sites. One of their ambulances was permanently located at Lipovac. They also helped to transport patients requiring advanced medical attention to the main hospital in Vukovar. Indomedcoy worked hard to foster close ties with local communities and was even actively involved with the football team in Dali.

Displaced Persons and Refugees

Beginning in 1991, thousands of people were displaced from their homes and had settled in the Region. There were thousands of displaced persons in Osijek, Vinkovci and other cities. Concerning those in the UNTAES Region, the Erdut Agreement noted that all persons, who came to the Region having previous permanent residence in Croatia, had the right to remain in the Region or return to their homes of origin.

The UN High Commissioner for Refugees (UNHCR) was the primary individual responsible for assisting displaced persons and refugees. Other Non-Governmental Organizations (NGOs) worked with UNHCR. UNTAES set the framework and assisted those organizations with their tasks.

UNTAES provided information about obtaining Domovnica and Croatian ID cards, and about registering with the Office of Displaced Persons and Refugees (ODPR). ODPR was the Croatian Government Office responsible for all displaced persons throughout Croatia. All such people had equal rights to assistance. People within the UNTAES Region used ODPR services in Ilok, Vukovar and Beli Manastir.

UNTAES had six Civil Affairs Offices located in Beli Manastir, Erdut, and Ilok, Osijek, Vinkovci and Vukovar. In each office, there was a Civil Affairs Officer who specialized in assistance and information for displaced persons and provided forms to request village visits or to help people return to their homes. UNTAES also worked to help people find the opportunities to return to their homes in other sections of Croatia.

Fry-Croatia Normalize Relations

The President of the Republic of Serbia, Slobodan Milosevic, and the President of the Republic of Croatia, Franjo Tudjman, met in Athens on August 7th and held comprehensive talks about the promotion of the peace process in the region and normalization of relations between the two States. In the Joint Communiqué about the talks, it was noted that there was readiness to "fully normalize relations" between the two countries and "to establish and develop good relations between their citizens and peoples".

Regarding the UNTAES Region, the Communiqué stressed support for the UN Administration, the "need to consistently implement" the Basic Agreement and "to refrain from all deeds and actions which could compromise the consistent and full compliance with the agreement.

Regarding refugees and displaced persons, the parties stated they were "ready to create conditions for the free and safe return of all such people to the places of origin which they freely chose".

The statement also noted the agreement to exchange immediately all available information about missing persons, the desire to solve the issue of Prevlaka through bilateral talks and to deal with issues of private property, pensions and other such issues. The Foreign Ministers of both countries met in Belgrade soon after to "sign the Agreement on the Normalization of Mutual Relations". The Joint Communiqué further strengthened the process of peaceful integration of the Region and was in accord with the provisions of both the Basic Agreement and Security Counsel Resolution 1037.

Athens Joint Communique Highlights

The communiqué announced the normalization of relations between the two states. It expressed readiness to create the conditions for the free and safe return of all refugees and displaced persons to their places of origin or other places that they freely chose.

It noted that safe return implied general amnesty.

It announced the decision to accelerate, without delay, the resolution of the issue of missing persons.

It pledged that the parties would prevent or refrain from all deeds and actions that could compromise the consistent and full compliance with the Erdut Agreement.

The two Presidents expressed their full support for the implementation of the provisions of the Dayton Agreement signed in Paris.

Summer Camp Underway for Children

A Summer Camp organized by local authorities, teachers and UN-TAES began in Ilok and Beli Manastir. About 50 students from both towns participated at camps located at local schools. For many children, the weeklong camp was the first they had attended in several years. Educational and sporting activities, evening campfires and visits to historical sites were some of the recreational programs organized on a daily basis.

The United Kingdom's Foreign Office made a donation of $10,000 U.S. dollars for the program.

Ms. Nobes handing over the money

Happy faces at the camp

An attaché from the British Embassy in Zagreb, Paula Nobes, said the British Ambassador, who visited the Region once a month, picked it from a list of various projects requiring funding from Jacques Klein's office in Vukovar. Ms Nobes said they were happy to contribute to the cost. Children between the ages of 15 and 17 years formed the first group. This was followed by two other sessions for children 12-15 and for younger groups. In all, about 300 children enjoyed the experience of the summer camp.

Monthly Salaries for Civil Servants

The first payment of monthly salaries was made to 127 Regional civil servants on August 8 in Borovo-Nasalje. The salaries were funded by a grant of 6 million Kunas provided earlier by the Croatian Government. The Croatian Government also agreed to provide five monthly install-ments of 4.5 million Kunas, to be paid between August 10 and January 15, 1997. The funds went towards meeting local government adminis-trative costs in the UNTAES Region.

CHAPTER 10

REGIONAL LEADERS IN ZAGREB

Jacques, accompanied by 20 Regional leaders, traveled to Zagreb on August 29, for face-to-face meetings with Croatian leaders and other government officials. After meeting with Croatian Deputy Prime Minister Ivica Kostovic, the delegation split into various working groups to discuss issues of health care, education, economics and social services with their counterparts.

Asked how the meeting came about Jacques said, "During my meetings with the Regional Assembly, as well as with the Executive Council, I said that what they needed to do was to address their concerns directly to Croatian Government officials. I suggested that I could fly them to Zagreb, where they could seriously begin discussions on whatever ethnic, religious, language, education or cultural autonomy they wanted and that's how it happened."

Jacques and Mr. Kostovic talking to the press at ferry event

International donors respond to funding call

Economic development was an important factor in bringing about stability in the UNTAES Region and building confidence among the population. All sides understood the urgency of economic revitalization to be an essential part of the reintegration process.

The Economic Reconstruction and Coordination Unit (ERCU) was created within UNTAES to identify urgent infrastructure and other projects and promote funding for these projects. Several international donors responded to the ERCU appeal for funding. The U. S. Agency for International Development (USAID) programmed 16 million US dollars through 1998 for different project areas in municipal rehabilitation, economic revitalization and civil rights and humanitarian programs. The Belgian Government offered $1.5 million for reconstruction projects of which $1 million was earmarked for the rehabilitation of the Port of Vukovar.

Another sum of $400,000 was given to the Belgian Red Cross for medical assistance in the Region. The Norwegian Government and its aid agencies pledged $1.8 million for reconstruction of schools, repairs of water wells and housing reconstruction in villages selected by UNHCR.

Among the largest donors was the European Commission based in Brussels. As the executive body of the European Union, EC accomplished all necessary procedures for allocation of the funds in less time than usual and announced on 29 July that it has agreed to provide funds totaling nearly $14 million for economic development and reconstruction of the Region. Four project areas were addressed immediately: the water supply network in and around Vukovar, the electricity supply network, removal of ruins and debris and restoration of a number of police stations in and around Vukovar.

For these projects the EC earmarked the equivalent of $ 7.85 million. A second allocation of $5.28 million was for projects involving the return of refugees and displaced persons in coordination with UNHCR.

A third allocation of about $857,000 actually came from ECHO (European Commission Humanitarian Organization). This was for three projects: the first was the main water supply network in Vukovar, the second was for pumps and dykes in Baranja and the third was an overall project for all the villages of the region to repair and restore infrastructure.

Some donors made direct contributions to the UNTAES Trust Fund. They were: USAID -$900,000, Sweden -$100,000, Belgium - $50,000 and Norway -$20,000. These funds formed a base from which UNTAES could allocate funds on specific projects at its discretion.

Civil Rights Project

The Civil Rights Project (CRP), an independent nongovernmental organization (NGO) funded by the United States and Norway, provided legal information and assistance to people living in the UNTAES Region as well as to people who wished to return to the Region. Because, under the terms of the Erdut Agreement, the Region will, at the end of the UNTAES mandate period, come under the full legal authority of Croatia. CRP assisted people in the protection of their human and civil rights with regards to various issues pertaining to their legal status in Croatia. Through its staff of international attorneys, attorneys qualified in Croatian law, and attorneys who resided in the Region, CRP provided information and assistance concerning such legal issues as:

Croatian citizenship-CRP provided information and assistance regarding procedures for obtaining citizenship for persons who simply needed their citizenship confirmed, as well as for persons who wished to become naturalized citizens. CRP also provided information about the legal rights that went along with Croatian citizenship;

Retrieval of personal documents-CRP provided information and assistance regarding the replacement or retrieval of personal documents such as birth certificates, marriage certificates, and workbooks; through a network of local NGOs, CRP assisted people with the retrieval of personal documents left behind in places of prior residence in Croatia;

Property-CRP provided information about property issues, including information about Croatian law on the sale and transfer of property.

Pensions-CRP provided information about the eligibility requirements and procedures for obtaining pensions paid by the Croatian Government as well as information and assistance about the retrieval of documents verifying a person's past work history in Croatia.

CRP had offices in Vukovar, Beli Manistir and Osijek.

<u>World Health Organization</u>

The World Health Organization is a UN agency whose mandate is to provide support in the field of health. The WHO has been active in the Region since the start of 1993. The WHO implemented programs involving community based physical rehabilitation, mental health and public health. WHO professionals held regular seminars and workshops with their local counterparts to define the needs and strategies for implementing the models they drew up for these programs.

The WHO, working with UNTAES medical resources and the UNHCR, provided essential drugs to all health institutions in the Region, as well as specialized kits including anesthesiology or special vaccines upon request.

The WHO monitored the overall health situation in the Region. It completed a survey of the health system in the Region in July and distributed it to all parties concerned.

<u>Register Your Weapons</u>

Demilitarization in the Region had a positive impact. One could walk around towns and villages without seeing weapons and not being stopped at checkpoints. This was the first and certainly most important step in returning to a normal life. This meant a peaceful society, where human rights and law and order would be respected.

UNTAES, through its military presence in the Region and the presence of the Transitional Police Force, worked hard to develop a peaceful society. In the same spirit and aimed toward the same goal, UNTAES announced a registration procedure for weapons to be legally retained by the civilian population.

Which weapons can you keep?

You cannot possess weapons that belong to the following categories: automatic weapons such as Kalashnikov; semiautomatic weapons with cartridges of 10 rounds and more; weapons equipped with a silencer; weapons that expel explosive projectiles; all kinds of explosive devices; ammunition with exploding, flammable or toxic projectiles; and other weapons of a purely military nature. Other personal and hunting weapons may be legally registered.

How can you keep your weapons?

Under specific conditions you were permitted to keep your weapon(s) and have them registered if they were used to ensure your personal protection or for the purpose of hunting or sporting.

A weapon certificate of registration was required for possession of self-defense weapons. For hunting, as for sporting, a permit to carry a weapon was required. The weapons registered for hunting/sporting could be carried within a 10-km radius of your residence. All previously issued authorizations to carry weapons automatically became invalid, regardless of issuing authority.

What is the procedure?

Individuals were required to bring their weapon(s) to be registered to the Police station closest to their residence. Applications had to be completed for each weapon one wished to keep. If all legal requirements were met, the registration certificate was immediately delivered. Should an investigation be deemed necessary, people were given a receipt for the weapon they brought for registration and the weapon was kept at the Police station, pending the results of the investigation. The same procedure was applied to get a permit for hunting and sporting weapons.

What conditions must be met?

In order to obtain a registration document the following requirements had to be met: the weapon was authorized, the reason for possession justified, the applicant was 18 years old, the applicant had not been found guilty of a crime or misdemeanor, there were no circumstances which indicated that the weapon could be abused; the applicant was in good mental and physical health.

Institutions also must register their weapons

Civilian institutions (organizations, firms, private companies) could also possess weapons in order to protect their own property. The individuals, employed by the institution and for whose use the weapon(s) was intended, had to meet the same conditions as for other citizens and show the necessity to keep weapons to defend the property.

The principle of not allowing weapons in public remained in force. The private security companies were not authorized to employ armed guards but could ensure the protection of civilian institutions by using the weapons registered and kept within the installations of the concerned institutions.

Useful information

The carrying of a weapon, registered or not, outside of the home; the carrying of a hunting or sporting weapon outside of the legal limit or the mere possession of an unregistered weapon were all violations of law and could be prosecuted. Such violations could lead to confiscation of weapons, substantial fines and even imprisonment.

The UNTAES Force had the right to detain anyone carrying a weapon in public and to seize the prohibited weapon.

ACT AS A RESPONSIBLE CITIZEN AND REGISTER YOUR WEAPONS AT THE NEAREST POLICE STATION

Mending Broken Bridges

When the Klisa-Osijek road was opened on July 25th, little did anyone imagine that around the ruins of a broken overpass and within the former Zone of Separation, people separated by war would cross over from their sides in such large numbers to meet with each other and re-establish contact. The market and meeting place in the former Zone of Separation on the Klisa-Osijek highway was first opened to the public on August 24th between 0800 and 1200. The event was not widely advertised because it was arranged on short notice. However, more than 200 people from both sides attended, giving UNTAES organizers cause for optimism about continuing the effort.

A family meets again

Jacques talking to the populace

…and the people came…

A few days before I departed the Mission, we were able to convince the Croatian government to come to the Zone of Separation where the two sides had been meeting each Saturday. Our goal was to have them tear down the cement bridge that had been blown up during the war and remove the rubble. Finally, one weekday morning, they arrived to begin demolition. As they began to clear the debris, a terrible explosion occurred, killing seven Croatian workers. The place where we had walked every weekend for almost a year had covered a deep land mine...one that could only be triggered by heavy equipment or a tank. It was a shock and caused all of us to think long and hard about how close we had come to dying.

Emotional Reunion

Periodically, I was quoted in newspaper, radio and TV reports in the Region. During one of the reunions, I was asked about our efforts of working with the Red Cross. It was an emotional moment, even though we had all gotten hardened to the realities of the chaos in which we were living.

"We had the idea of expanding on what the Red Cross had been doing for family reunions" said UNTAES spokesman Temple Black. "We wanted something spontaneous, where people and vendors from both sides could come out and deal with each other. We wanted families and friends to call each other on the phone and say 'Let's drive down and meet at this place'."

On August 31st, there were 2800 people at the meeting place and then, as word spread. A record number of 5880 people (3220 from other parts of Croatia and 2660 from the Region) plus 24 vendors (8 from Osijek and 16 from the Region) came on September 7th.

This showed us that the people were ahead of their leadership because we had local official resistance to holding the event. We were also told that nobody would show up for the event.

Because of the great success we had, we planned to expand the number of market events. On September 10th, 8,000 people attended the market meeting place event. Interestingly, there was no problem with regard to currency dealings, as people freely traded in Kunas and Dinars. The Croatian Company, Saponia, set up an outdoor café outside the former Zone of Separation and the Slavonska Bank from Osijek operated a currency exchange service. The exchange markets continued with great success.

Vendors doing a brisk business

Time to relax and talk

Needs assessment survey

As more and more projects for the development of the Region were arranged, there was a strong need to identify all those areas where reconstruction and rehabilitation was required, both in the short and long term. The Civil Affairs office of UNTAES launched a house-to-house survey of the Region for this purpose.

The survey was aimed at getting answers to questions on the number of people in a family, their present occupations and sources of income, details on property ownership in 1990 and at present and their plans for the future.

Strictly Confidential

International UN volunteers under the overall supervision of UNTAES Civil Affairs conducted the survey. We stressed that this was not a registration of people. There was no reference to individual identities in the questionnaire. No names of the head of the family or family members were asked or noted in the survey.

The idea of carrying out a needs assessment survey was discussed by the Joint Implementation Committee (JIC) on Refugees and Displaced Persons. The Serb delegation had identified 21 villages and towns, such as Vukovar and Ilok, which had a significant population of displaced persons and refugees. Mayors in the Region had already been requested to inform their populations about the data collection process and they promised their full support in encouraging people to cooperate fully with survey teams in the field. A pilot survey project was successfully completed in Sarengrad.

Collected data was strictly confidential and anonymous and was used by UNTAES only as a statistical base for negotiations with the international community and the Croatian Government to secure maximum protection and rehabilitation benefits for people of the Region.

Stanimirovic and Seks talk as Jacques, Boothby and Fischer look on

On September 9th, the Federal Republic of Yugoslavia and the Republic of Croatia exchanged notes in Zagreb and Belgrade on the basis of Article 3 of the Agreement on the Normalization of Relations, establishing full diplomatic and consular relations and raising the existing missions to the level of embassies.

A Croatian Parliamentary Delegation headed by Vladimir Seks visited UNTAES headquarters in Vukovar on September 10th to hold talks with Serb representatives in the Region. Jacques Klein was present at the talks.

The delegation later traveled to Ilok, Djeletovci and Lipovac. Another delegation led by Croatian Prime Minister Zlatko Matesa also visited the Region that same afternoon.

UN High Commisioner for Refugees

The UNHCR's relief effort in the region of former Yugoslavia began in October 1991 when the UN Secretary-General designated UNHCR as the lead agency for UN humanitarian relief operations in the former Yugoslavia. There were 27 UNHCR offices in former Yugoslavia that provided humanitarian assistance and protection to some 3.1 million refugees, displaced persons and war affected persons.

In the UNTAES Region, UNHCR provided humanitarian assistance to 60,000 displaced Serbs who fled Western Slavonia and former UN Sectors North and South after military operations were carried-out in 1995.

UNHCR shifted its emphasis following the signing of the Dayton and Erdut agreements from emergency relief to a search for durable solutions for displaced persons by helping them to return to their homes. In the UNTAES Region, UNHCR was lead agency for the issue of the return of displaced persons and chaired the UNTAES Joint Implementation Committee on returns.

In order to develop confidence-building measures, the UNHCR designated pilot projects for the return of displaced persons to three villages in Eastern Slavonia and Baranja (Aritunovac, Ernestinovo, Bilje) and one village in Western Slavonia (Kusonje). In addition, UNTAES arranged other projects for the return of displaced persons in cooperation with UNHCR.

UNHCR also financed and coordinated the activities of various NGOs, which worked on the reconstruction of public buildings, basic infrastructure and private houses in its villages. Other UNHCR implementing agencies sponsored programs of social welfare and support for the population in the Region.

Japan Emergency NGO's

JEN is a consortium of seven different Japanese NGOs, which initially came to the former Yugoslavia and particularly the Region, in May 1994 on a needs assessment survey.

The program revealed many urgent needs, but what caught their attention was the acute lack of medicines for displaced persons in the Region. So JEN decided to address this problem by opening a pharmacy in Vukovar.

JEN began on August 25, 1994 by providing medical assistance to refugees, pensioners and needy families in the area. From the initial number of 20 to 25 patients who came in daily, the number increased to about 150. JEN also provided medical assistance on a regular monthly basis to the Old Folks Home in Sarengrad.

In 1995, JEN listed a total of 16,000 beneficiaries. The figure for the first eight months of 1996 was already more than 20,000 people. As Dr. Raja Channel, who heads the JEN operation in the Region proudly said, "Excepting holidays, we were open every single day, even during the most difficult and tense periods." On average, medicines worth approximately US $20,000 were dispensed every month. JEN coordinated with UNHCR and WHO in order to avoid duplication of their work.

In March 1996, following a request made by UNHCR, JEN established their presence in the Baranja by opening a pharmacy in Bell Monastic, and from August 21st, with the acquisition of two mobile pharmacy vehicles, JEN reached out to people in Ilok, Loaves, Tovarnik, Bapska, Tenja, Silas and Markusica.

An interesting aspect of JENs work in the area is the annual distribution of a gift bag for children, which is sent from Japan by one of the organizations represented in JEN. In 1994, more that 8,000 students in the Region were presented with this special bag containing toys, books, sketchpads, pencils, pens, greeting cards, etc. In 1995, 11,000 such bags were distributed. For 1996, 15 Japanese student volunteers traveled to the Region for seven days and distributed an estimated 15,000 bags in the Region, including the Baranja.

The Document Center

The Document Center Staff

More than 4,000 persons applied for Croatian documents at the four offices in Beli Manastir, Batina, Ilok and Vukovar. Of these, nearly 2,000 applications were to obtain citizenship papers and the rest were for Birth Certificates, Identification Cards and Passports.

When applying, people were told to bring their birth certificate, their old SFRY Licna Carta, or any other official documents they had available. Even if they did not have any documents, they could still apply.

The Croatian Government did not charge any fees for issuing documents. They were available free. People did not have to give up their personal documents in order to obtain Croatian documents. They could keep their documents as long as they remained valid.

CHAPTER 11

WEAPONS BUY-BACK PROGRAM

When I first heard about the weapons buy back program, I thought it was an ingenious idea to help get guns off the streets of Vukovar and the Region. What neither I, nor anyone else realized was that the people we were dealing with had more weapons than we could afford. It turns out that they were selling us weapons, many times, from world war two. These were weapons that had been buried long before we arrived and were literally just collecting dust in a hole somewhere. It was a pretty good scam they were running on us, almost a good as the Russian troops stealing U.N. gasoline and selling it on the streets to the local Serbs.

Demilitarization of the Region was one of the first and most important tasks of the UNTAES mandate defined under UN Security Council resolution 1037. This element of the mandate, which involved the removal of heavy weapons like tanks, mortars and artillery pieces from the Region, was successfully completed by June 21.

UNTAES followed this with a "weapons registration program" where people were encouraged to come forward and register their personal and hunting weapons.

In the third phase of normalization, UNTAES, in cooperation with the Croatian Government, launched a unique "Weapons Buy-Back

Scheme" aimed at removing offensive weapons and ammunition from the Region so that people could continue with their lives, free from any fear or threat. Two significant factors in the "Buy-Back" scheme were: the assurance of total anonymity and an attractive on the spot cash payment for goods received. Here's a Q&A we used to explain the program.

Q. What is a weapons Buy-Back scheme?

A. UNTAES, in cooperation with the Croatian Government has drawn up a list of certain weapons, ammunition and explosives, which you can bring to collection points and exchange for on-the-spot cash.

Q. I did not register some of my weapons under the registration program. Can I bring such weapons under the Buy-Back scheme?

A. Yes. Anyone can bring his weapons, ammunition and explosives under this scheme without fear. If you have some weapons that are not on the list, you can still inquire with the military experts at the receiving points if they will buy those weapons. However, land mines of any kind will not be accepted under this scheme... they are too dangerous.

Q. Do I have to bring my ID for the exchange?

A. No ID is required and no names will be asked. The whole procedure of taking your weapons, evaluating its price and making payment in cash will be anonymous. "

Q. Where can I take my weapons to sell?

A. There are four UNTAES points. In the Baranja, you can go to Belgian Battalion in Beli Manastir or Pakistani Battalion in Topolik. In the southern part of the Region, it is the Russian Battalion in Klisa and Jordanian Battalion in Grabovo. They operated between 0900 and 1600 hours.

Q. How were weapons evaluated?

A. Croatian and UNTAES military experts listed certain weapons present in the Region and their general value. The price was estimated on the basis of the condition of the weapon. For example, a good condition, automatic rifle like the M-70 Crvena Zastava could have been worth about 550 Kunas or 155 DEM. The prices for all weapons and other items was reduced in proportion to their level of defect or condition.

Q. Who paid for the weapons and in what currency were they paid?

A. This plan was worked together with the Croatian Government and they were paid in DEM until mid-October and in Kunas thereafter.

Q. How long did the program remain open?

A. The "Buy-Back" began on October 2nd and continued until January 5, 1997.

Knezevo - Udvar Border Opened

Another step towards opening up the Region to the outside world, and assisting in its peaceful reintegration with the rest of Croatia, was taken on October 4th when the ceremonial ribbon to declare the Knezevo-Udvar border crossing open. Present at the occasion were delegations from the Croatian and Hungarian Governments.

The opening was made possible following signing of the Protocol between UNTAES, the Government of Croatia and-the Government of Hungary on September 26, 1996.

At present the crossing will be opened between 0800 and 1600 hours for the following persons:

Residents of the UNTAES administered Region who have Croatian or Hungarian passports;

Vehicles from the UNTAES Region who have registered travel documents issued by the Croatian Government; and, Vehicles registered by the Hungarian government with travel documents.

Vehicles with RSK license plates were not allowed to enter or return from Hungary through this border crossing point.

Another significant step is that commercial buses and their passengers, bearing either Hungarian travel documents or Croatian passports or travel documents, can cross the Knezevo-Udvar border crossing point and transit through the Region to other places in Croatia and return.

Residents of the UNTAES Region having Croatian passports can use these buses to enter and return from Hungary. Residents of the Region with Croatian ID cards or Domovnica will be able to ride on these buses to go to Osijek and back.

The border crossing point on the Knezevo side is under UNTAES control and the Transitional Police Force (TPF) will perform all police functions associated with the crossing. The functioning of the border crossing point will be reviewed after 30 days by the delegation of experts from the Croatian and Hungarian Governments and UNTAES, and will make changes if necessary and mutually agreeable.

More than 6,000 weapons Bought-Back

When the UNTAES weapons "Buy- Back" program was announced, nobody was sure of how it would turn out because this was something new and untried. There were many questions about the scheme in general but mainly, it was related to the situation in the Region. Did people believe that the conflict in the Region was truly over? If they did, would people come for the prices being offered? After an initial hesitancy, people began queuing up at the four designated weapons "Buy-

Back "places in the Region when they opened on October 2nd. Word had spread that there really was nothing to fear as the whole procedure was as simple and anonymous as UNTAES had promised.

Each day at the four collection points was different. Some days only a few rifles turned up. On other occasions, so much equipment came in that the Croatian representatives ran out of cash by early afternoon.

A storage depot at RUSBAT Headquarters

In fact, one day, two men brought in about 70 anti-tank rocket launchers. At the declared price of 155 Deutsche Marks per piece, they were paid 10,850DEM.

This actually encouraged the Croatian Government to widen the scope of items under the Buy-Back scheme from a limited initial list, to include many other categories of weapons and explosives with the exception of mines. Approximately 6,000 weapons, including over 2,300 portable anti-tank rocket launchers were received for payment of about 500,000 DEM. As announced earlier, the "Buy-Back" is now reimbursed in Kunas. The collected items are taken away to UNTAES storage sites where after sorting, items which are not in the best of condition, they are destroyed by UNTAES ordnance experts under controlled conditions. Other weapons are put in UNTAES storage depots. The destruction of ammunition under the Buy-Back scheme is being carried out in a secluded swamp area called Aljmaski Rit, between Aljmas and Marinovci farm. Except for slight shock waves in the immediate vicinity, there was no danger to people or property.

Ready for demolition

Loans for Small Enterprises

Following a grant of $ 3 million dollars from the United States Agency for International Development (USAID), the Monetary Osijek Agency (MOA) opened its office in Osijek on October 21, 1996. Jacques, the US ambassador to Croatia, Peter Galbraith, and Ms. Barbara Turner of USAID in Washington, were present on the occasion.

Aimed at economic revitalization through encouraging small businesses, the MOA disbursed loans for projects costing between $1,000 and $20,000 at low-interest rates. The focus was primarily on supporting agriculture related activities, small production lines like bakeries and service oriented enterprises.

The operating area was in Pozega, Slavonski Brod, Osijek, Vinkovci, and Baranja. All those who fulfilled the conditions were eligible for loans. As soon as certain legal procedures were established, there were plans to open two credit offices in Vukovar and Baranja, to receive applications from within the UNTAES Region.

Agreement on Agriculture

On October 15th, Jacques presided over the signing ceremony of the Memorandum of Understanding (MOU) that addressed economic issues concerning Regional agriculture. The MOU was signed by Dr. Vojislav Stanimirovic on behalf of the local Serb leadership and by Mr. Mirko Tankosic of the Croatian Government. The memorandum, while integrating parts of agriculture companies from the UNTAES Region into the economic system of the Republic of Croatia, also provided for interest-free credits for the fall planting in the Region. The value of the interest-free credits for the farmers' land amounted to 1083.30 Kunas per hectare. Repayment of the equivalent value was made by wheat deliveries in 1997.

The memorandum identified participants of these arrangements on both sides. Managements of the joint stocks companies Belje, IPK and Vupik and of the organizing units of the same companies in the UNTAES Region jointly followed and monitored the progress of the fall planting.

The Regional organizing units of IPK, Belje and VUPIK companies were credited with 350 kg of mineral fertilizer and 30 liters of diesel per hectare. Repayment was made in wheat or cash.

Deminers from Region Undergo Leadership Training

A three-week leadership training program on de-mining for 15 students from the UNTAES Region was carried out from October 6-23rd in the mountains of Brus, between Sarajevo and Pale in Bosnia. Funded by the American Government, the three-phase training program covered leadership skills, equipment and demolition training and minefield reconnaissance/clearing.

Jacques, accompanied by Dr. Vojislav Stanimirovic traveled to the location to get a first-hand impression of the training process. "I think everyone understands the de-mining problem in Eastern Slavonia is significant," Klein said. "The pay-off of this training is long term because these men will be busy for years doing something very, very useful. And that is making the region safe for children and other people who live there. "

Dr. Stanimirovic said it is very important that people get the education in humanitarian de-mining which is somewhat different from military de-mining. "Courageous people need to do it. There is no place for heroes in the minefields, only for professionals and bold ones, "he said. Dr. Stanimirovic also thanked the United States for making the money and the experts from the US Special Forces team available. Special kits valued at between $3,000-4,000 were given to each student upon completion of the course.

World Health Organization Announces Opening of Two Offices for Issuing Croatian Health Insurance Cards

On October 10, 1996 two offices of the Croatian health insurance Institute started operating in Vukovar and Beli Manistir. Both offices were located within the compound of the UNTAES document centers. In each office, there was one team of two Croatian administrators from the Croatian Health Insurance Institute of Vinkovci and Osijek.

The issuance of a Croatian Health Insurance booklet to the inhabitants of the Region was an important step toward peaceful reintegration of the Regional Health system into the Croatian health system.

Those persons with a Croatian ID and Domovnica were entitled to register with the Croatian health insurance system, which provided full medical coverage to the population, from primary health care to hospital referral.

Dr. Stephan Turek, Director of the National Health Insurance Institute based in Zagreb, contributed to   this successful operation. At the same time, Regional Serb health professionals guaranteed health care access and equity to every inhabitant of the region, regardless of their health insurance status.

The main goal of the WHO was to ensure health for all. National compulsory health insurance was seen as a step toward this goal. During the UNTAES period, there were two systems of health insurance running in parallel, the Regional Serb and Croatian system. Eventually, one system, the Croatian Health Insurance System, prevailed. Consequently, WHO encouraged inhabitants of the Region to get the Croatian health insurance card, if they qualified.

No Change for Border Crossings

A transitional customs and immigration service similar to the Transitional Police Force was established. This followed an agreement between the Director of the Croatian Customs Service and his counterpart in the Region, to hold joint training sessions for customs officers. The transitional customs and immigration service operated during the course of the UNTAES mandate, after which it was fully integrated under Croatian law and regulations.

With regard to the movement of people from and into the Region, there was no change from the existing system. Visas were not required and people were free to cross the borders using the documents they had been using.

Following the normalization agreement signed between Croatia and the Federal Republic of Yugoslovia in September, delegations from the two governments negotiated a variety of bilateral matters, including payment of pensions, health systems and visa requirements for their citizens.

Truck inspection at the Batina Bridge

Under his authority as Transitional Administrator, Klein instructed all international border crossings between the Region, Hungary and the Federal Republic of Yugoslavia, mainly Batina, Udvar, Erdut, Ilok and Tovarnik be closed to commercial traffic from 1900 to 0700 hours. This measure was introduced to curb smuggling and illegal transportation of commercial goods from the Region and did not affect personal movement of people and vehicles between 1900 and 0700 hours.

Croatia and the Council of Europe---what it meant

Ms Claudia Luciani, Directorate of Political Affairs of the Council of Europe in Strasbourg, visited Vukovar to participate in a human rights seminar for Serb and Croat Displaced Persons. Her work dealt mainly with the republics of the former Yugoslavia, but also covered other countries such as Albania and Bulgaria. The republics of the former Yugoslavia, Slovenia and Former Yugoslav Republic of Macedonia were already members of the Council of Europe. On November 6, 1996 Croatia became the 40th member of the Council. Here, Ms. Luciani discussed the criteria for membership, and the obligations and rewards of being part of the Council.

Q. Since 1992, Croatia had sought admission to the Council of Europe. What criteria were used to determine admission?

A. The criteria used for admitting Croatia were the same used for every candidate member. That is, that every member must respect three fundamental conditions: human rights, rule of law, and pluralist democracy. In addition, we ask the country that becomes a member to sign, and within a year to ratify, the European Convention on human rights and to accept the supervision of the control bodies of the Convention, the Commission and the Court. The country must also accept that individuals can apply directly to Strasbourg control bodies. That means the country loses, in a way, its sovereignty in respect to human rights. This means that the Strasbourg bodies can investigate complaints and can ultimately condemn a country and it's Government for any violation. Or it can ask the Government to remedy the violation either financially or by changing the laws etc. The member country essentially accepts international supervision of its activities in these areas.

Q. Six months ago when it was denied access to the Council of Europe, there were certain conditions put to Croatia. Does acceptance now mean the conditions have been met?

A. We are not saying the country has fulfilled them all and that it is a perfect democracy because none of the Member States is a perfect democracy. What Council of Europe membership means is that the country is truly committed to achieving these goals.

Positive role

Q. What convinced the Member States to accept Croatia as a new member?

A. I think what was critical in the decision was that the Government had agreed to some of the points and had actually made progress on some points like the amnesty law, the media law, and had in general shown a cooperative and positive attitude to the various requests that were made. Also, it was recognized by most of the States that Croatia had played a positive role in the elections in Bosnia.

In the case of Croatia, and specific to Croatia, another very decisive factor was that the political opposition, the Serbs living here and some of the other groups that were not in power said they were in favor of Croatia's accession to the Council of Europe. By having Croatia even more integrated into this system of protection of human rights, these groups felt they would be more secure in their rights.

Q. The Council of Europe is neither a military nor an economic organization. What mechanisms of control can the Council exert on its members to keep them in conformity with their commitments?

A. The ultimate sanction is expulsion. It has actually only happened once in the case of Greece in the years in which Greece was under dictatorship. Greece was suspended from the organization, and when a new constitution was adopted and democracy restored, Greece was readmitted to the Council of Europe. So this ultimate sanction was used only in a clear and blatant case of deviation from the agreed upon standards of the Council of Europe (CoE).

Another method of control exerted upon the members is the monitoring of commitments by the countries themselves. The CoE also relies on information received from respected NGOs, international organizations, ambassadors, and media sources throughout Europe.

In addition to the monitoring system, the Council of Europe has a parliamentary assembly, which can take up a controversial issue and discuss it openly during the sessions. In such a way, by discussing issues in public, the Council of Europe can exert some pressure on member states to conform to the standards to which they agreed.

Benefits

Q. What are the benefits of membership? Why would a country want to be a member of this organization, signing agreements that require its constitution, legislation and behavior towards its citizens be subject to international scrutiny without any military or economic benefits in return?

A. Essentially, for countries like Croatia, this is a political recognition that they have come a certain way towards fulfilling the principles of democracy and human rights and now belong to the respected club of the European countries, which are committed to the same values. I think it was an important recognition internationally.

For most of the countries of central and Eastern Europe, membership is seen as a first step towards membership in the European Union, which is definitely the ultimate goal of most of these European countries. And, in a way, it does serve as an entrance to the EU because while a member of the Council of Europe, the members are also working on inter-governmental structures, meeting their colleagues, and explaining the positions of their Government. In that sense, it is a very useful tool to a country.

Djeletovci gas reconnected to Jankovci

On October 25th, gas from the Djeletovci oil fields once again flowed into the pipeline towards the headquarters of the Jankovci Farmers Association. This followed several weeks of negotiations between Industrial Nafte (INA), the Croatian state-owned oil company, and the consumer organizations in Jankovci, led by the Farmers Association. The significance of this to the Jankovci community is tremendous. As Mr. Popovic, Director of the Jankovci Farmers Association said, "This means that the 50,000 tons of corn in storage can be dried here instead of in Serbia. The transportation costs saved in this manner will help keep the price of grain low."

A few meters away, the Jankovci brick factory too had much to gain from the re-supply of gas. Since April, when the gas pipes from Djeletovci were closed, the factory had been running on diesel, which increased costs by two and half times. This action forced them to layoff more than 100 workers.

Another heartening aspect of gas supply being restored was that the contemplated closure of the Jankovci primary school was averted. As central heating of the school was gas-run, the Jankovci community planned to close the school during winter. The gas supply had eased the worry of parents and students. Technicians from INA had earlier inspected the pipelines to ensure that there was no leakage and that the required pressure could be maintained. Except for some missing gas meters, they found most of the system intact.

All gas produced from the Djeletovci oil fields (about 10,000-12,000 cubic meters per day) went to Jankovci. The required capacity for the Jankovci facilities was approximately 24,000 cubic meters per day and additional gas was made available by INA from Vinkovci as soon as some disconnected pipelines were fixed. There was so much goodwill and trust between the two parties, that the Jankovci community agreed to accept the meter readings from Djeletovci until such time as their own missing meters were replaced.

Flowers, candles and prayers for the departed souls

Displaced persons visit grave sites

More than 5,000 Croatian displaced persons (DP's) were able to visit the gravesites of their loved ones in the Region for the first time in five years on November 1st.

The visit on All Saints Day, a Catholic holy day, covered 30 villages and was observed in a solemn and dignified manner. The list of villages was drawn up by UNTAES in agreement with authorities on both sides marking another positive step in the reintegration process.

Local Serbs in various towns waved at busses carrying visitors and met with them in some locations.

About 40 buses, escorted by UN CIV Pol and the Transitional Police Force (TPF) brought in 2,000 people who were taken to 24 gravesites in the Baranja and in the Vukovar area. Another 3,000 people independently visited cemeteries in the Lipovac Corridor where recently, more open access for all Croatians had been established. There was not a single negative incident.

The association of DPs from both sides arranged the visits for their members. Reciprocal visits for Serbs from the Region to Western Slavonia were organized by UNTAES for November 2nd. Further visits of Serbs to other areas are planned.

CHAPTER 12

THE ERDUT AGREEMENT-UPDATE

The celebration at the Yellow House in Erdut was preceded by a bus tour of the Region. Ambassador Peter Galbraith wanted to see the progress that had been made and this was the most efficient means of achieving that objective. Since I had run many tour programs in my Air Force career, I volunteered to lead the program. We completed the tour exactly three-minutes behind schedule, prior to reaching the Yellow House. This was one of the "good days" in the Region.

UNTAES hosted a ceremony on November 12, 1996, commemorating the first anniversary of the signing of the Basic Agreement in Erdut. Ambassadors and envoys from the United States, France, the United Kingdom, Germany, Russia, Belgium, the Netherlands, Hungary, Norway, Canada, China, Greece, Italy, Spain, Pakistan, Turkey, Ukraine, Slovenia, Poland, Slovakia, the Czech Republic, as well as Croatian Government and local Serb leaders attended.

Jacques inspected a formal military Guard of Honor at the Yellow House, where the Basic Agreement between the Government of Croatia and the local Serb community had been signed in 1995.

Jacques and two of the principal architects of the agreement, Thorvald Stoltenberg of Norway and U. S. Ambassador to Croatia, Peter Gailbraith, spoke at the occasion.

Jacques and Ambassador Peter Gailbraith hold up the Plaque inscribing the Basic Agreement as Mr. Stoltenberg and Mr. Stanimirovich look on.

<u>Let's give peace a chance</u>

Jacques said the foundation for peace established by the Basic Agreement had enabled this mission to play a key role in forging a broader peace. "Eastern Slavonia had a strategic importance beyond its boundaries. UNTAES' success in demilitarizing the Region provided the environment in which the Governments of Croatia and the Federal Republic of Yugoslavia were able to normalize their relationship", he said. Klein noted that a Transitional Police Force had been established to oversee law and order, UNTAES had been able to reestablish communications between this Region and the rest of Croatia by opening roads, railways, waterways, telephone and communication systems, and that there were now five UN centers where people could apply and obtain Croatian documents.

Klein said that reconciliation was taking place at many levels. "On All Saints Day, we had over 5,000 visitors to the Region who paid their respects at the grave sites of their loved ones in a moving and dignified manner."

Force Commander General Schoups, Ambassador Galbraith, Jacques
and Mr. Stoltenberg

Since 24 August, more than 60, 000 people from far and wide had met
with each other at the weekly open-air market and meeting place operated by UNTAES between Klisa and Osijek. It showed that people
were ahead of their leaders in their desire to return to normalcy".

He said that the Serb leadership began moving forward in a significant
way, by participating in meetings in Zagreb between leading members
of the local Executive Council, led by Dr. Vojislav Stanimirovic, and
Croatian President Franjo Tudjman.

Ambassador Galbraith recalled the difficult negotiation process leading to the Agreement. He said that at the heart of the Agreement was
protecting the human rights of the people who lived in the Region
now, as well as those who had been forced to leave the Region during
the war.

"I am very much encouraged by President Tudjman's recent commitment to Dr. Stanimirovic that Croatia would treat its Serb citizens
equally, as I am also encouraged by Dr, Stanimirovic's public statement that the Serbs of this Region wish to be loyal citizens of Croatia,"
he said.

Pakbat Bagpipers provide an impressive escort.

Ambassador Gailbraith said that although there had been accomplishments, much remained to be done. "A lasting peace requires democracy and the cornerstone of democracy is pluralism and tolerance. Serb citizens of Croatia are entitled to the same rights as all other Croatians, including the right to practice their religion, to speak their own language, and to instruct their children about their own culture and history."

Mr. Galbraith also said that justice was essential to a lasting peace. In the past five years terrible crimes have been committed in Croatia and Bosnia and Herzegovina. "But we must remember that crimes are committed by individuals and not by peoples. Let us punish the guilty as a step to building reconciliation between peoples."

"Reconciliation also requires recognition that both Croats and Serbs had suffered in this war," Mr. Galbraith said. "No purpose can be served by asking who suffered more. Both communities have suffered. Neither community deserved what happened to it. Neither has a monopoly on being victimized."

In his speech Mr. Stoltenberg said that he could not have imagined a year ago that the situation in the Region could have progressed so well. In closing the ceremony Mr. Klein appealed for continued support from all concerned saying that the people of the Region deserved everyone's best efforts. He thanked everyone for their support and said: "Let's give peace a chance."

Security Council extends mandate

The United Nations Security Council extended the UNTAES mandate on 15 November. In a resolution adopted unanimously, the Council decided that the present mandate should continue to 15 July 1997 in its present form. The Council also decided that a UN "presence" should remain in the Region for a further six-month period. That presence may be a "restructured UNTAES" and will be decided later.

The resolution also makes clear that UNTAES has the responsibility to organize local elections in the Region. This action by the Council ensures that the secure step-by-step reintegration of the Region will continue at a faster pace during the coming months. Continuing and increased contact between local officials and Croatian Government authorities is essential to this effort.

Vinkovci-Sid train service ready to roll

There was renewed activity on the Vinkovci-Tovarnik railway line as Croatian Railways prepared for the opening of international rail traffic. Light repairs along the line had been carried out to clean up the road crossings and to add needed stone ballast in some places. Work had been undertaken to ensure that switches were operating or locked in the correct position. As many as five trains a day had been at work along the line between Mirkovci and Tovarnik, providing a welcome sight to residents of the Region and some surprises to passing motorists who had not seen trains for some time. Communication checks were carried out between the stations to determine the condition of the cables. In the absence of signals, these communications were an important means of controlling trains.

Although the line was ready to accept trains, the level was well below pre-war activity. The extensive damage to the electrical propulsion system, the signalization system, the stations and the road crossing barriers permitted only reduced operations, but the return of the trains signaled another step in the normalization of life in the Region.

Negotiations remained underway in the Joint Implementation Committee to finalize the method of re-employing the previous railway workers of the Region and reintegrating them into Croatian Railways. During the period of 28 October to 5 November as many workbooks as could be located were returned to former employees. Legal experts were present and answered many questions concerning eligibility for pensions and other personal requests for information. There was good cooperation by all concerned and everyone looked forward to the resumption of railway operations.

The Vinkovci-Sid railhead on the main line between Zagreb and Belgrade was an important link between central Europe and the south Balkans. The Orient Express the workers used to run on this line was a major hub of Croatian commercial traffic. Since the line was closed because of the war, people took alternate routes through Hungary, resulting in immeasurable loss to the future economies of both Croatia and the Federal Republic of Yugoslavia (FRY). With the normalization of relations and renewing between Croatia and FRY, this line expected to regain its former prominence as soon as the two States agreed upon modalities of border crossings.

Canadian Envoy lauds progress in the Region

Canada's Ambassador to Croatia, Graham Green, was among the foreign diplomats visiting the UNTAES Region. Mr. Green took part in ceremonies marking the first anniversary of the signing of the Basic Agreement.

People wanted to know what sort of interests and involvement Canada had in this part of the world. In fact, Canadians were among the first countries to send peacekeepers to Croatia. While Canada had very few troops in the UN or even IFOR operations based in Croatia, it did not mean that they were not interested in the peaceful reintegration of the Region. Canada felt that it was very important that Croatia be able to re-implement its administration here in a way that would allow all people who have the right under the Erdut Agreement, to stay in Croatia and feel comfortable and secure enough to want to stay. That's something that all of us involved in the search for peace in this Region support.

Institutions

Q. What are your impressions since your last visit to the Region?

A. I was very pleased to see the economic progress here, especially the steps UNTAES has taken with the local community and the Croatian Government to build the institutions. I was also here before with some of the people who had come to visit the graves of their loved ones for the first time in five years and was impressed at how people from both sides treated each other that day with respect and dignity.

Q. What gives Canada its reputation as a neutral peacekeeper?

A. The Canadians don't have a colonial past. They never had colonies, particularly like some permanent members of the Security Council. Canada has had a history as a peace keeping nation, sending its people to all parts of the world. They have always tried to find solutions in the best interests of the people of a particular Region. They had no vested interests in those regions. I think that sometimes makes Canadians more acceptable to parties in conflict. And that's why Canada has offered to lead the operation and contribute a battalion to the force going to Zaire and Rwanda.

Interesting Events

Six members of the local Serb Executive Council led by Dr. Vojislav Stanimirovic, met in Zagreb with Croatian President Franjo Tudjman and his senior aides, Government officials and leaders of Croatian displaced persons on 9 November. The meeting was arranged by UN-TAES and Jacques was present during the discussions. Another group accompanied Klein to Zagreb for meetings with Croatian leaders and Government officials on November 20. Volunteers representing a consortium of Japanese NGOs (JEN) traveled from Japan to the UN-TAES Region carrying gifts for school children.

From Japan with love

Dr. Rajeeb Khanal, who heads the JEN mission in Vukovar, said that this was an annual event and for the first time schools from the Baranja were also covered. The volunteers distributed more than 13,000 gift bags containing toys, books, pencils, crayons and other knick-knacks personally during the second week of November.

Donors Conference for Reconstruction

In an effort to accelerate the reconstruction of the Region and revitalize its economy, UNTAES hosted a Donor's Conference in Vukovar in early December. Preliminary meetings with Ambassadors and Envoys in Zagreb were held in October at which many countries promised their support. In his visits to several world capitals, Klein discussed with leaders the importance of economic reconstruction of the Region. "We all know that beginning the reconstruction of the Region is absolutely essential if we're going to maintain any stability", Klein said.

142

The Economic Reconstruction and Coordination Unit (ERCU) of UN-TAES identified several sectors such as Reconstruction, Education, Health, Agriculture Transport, Demining, etc., which required large funding. A list of priority projects for reconstruction and their cost estimates had been finalized. Emphasis had been placed on schemes aimed at small and medium businesses.

Unloading materials for rebuilding projects

The European Commission Humanitarian Office (ECHO) provided about $ 550,000 U.S. dollars for more than 34 small projects in the Region. These projects were implemented by GTZ, the German company contracted by ECHO for that purpose.

CHAPTER 13

E.C. RECONSTRUCTION HELP

Getting the Region back to normal was one of our highest priorities. We knew if we could get houses rebuilt, get the busses and trains to run on time and to show people things were getting back to normal, they would begin to believe that healing and growing was possible. These high-viz public events became paramount and quickly showed their impact on the local populace. Each successful event we accomplished led to the next positive accomplishment. They eventually built on themselves until such rare accomplishments became commonplace. Then we knew we were getting close to the end of our mission.

The UNTAES Civil Affairs office organized a "small community projects" program for the Region under the umbrella of the Economic Reconstruction and Coordinating Unit (ERCU). The program was aimed at providing equipment and materials to carry out urgent repairs to municipal electricity and water supply systems, as well as repairs to community centers, clinics and schools in villages. This also generated employment opportunities for local skilled labor.

We all knew that beginning reconstruction in the Region was absolutely essential. Throughout September and October, Civil Affairs field officers worked with local municipalities and experts in the Region to identify appropriate projects. An important factor in the selection was the cost range for each project. They had to be between

$10,000 - $30,000 dollars. A list of 34 projects was submitted to the European Community Humanitarian Office (ECHO), which allocated about $556,000 to cover the costs of the projects. ECHO, as its implementing agency for the projects, appointed a German firm, Deutsche Gesellschaft fuer Technische Zusarnmenarbeit.

In addition, ECHO made an additional allocation of $294,000 towards providing mobile water pumps for the Baranja region. GTZ had already purchased four pumps, which were delivered to the Belgian Battalion in Beli Manastir. Contracts were signed with 28 local contractors on October 30/31. The target date for completion of the projects was the end of November. ERCU was responsible for the overall coordination of the work.

Mr. Ghidi of ECHO inspecting a job with the GTZ representative

In the first two weeks of November, more than 40 trucks came to the Region with each truck carrying about 25 tons of reconstruction material. Civil Affairs, UN Civ Pol and the TPF coordinated the escort and delivery. Civil Affairs and representatives of GTZ constantly monitored the progress of the projects and reported back to the donor. Payments to contractors were made subject to certification by the GTZ. By early December all projects had been completed. Eighty additional projects were scheduled for completion during the following months.

President Tudjman visits the UNTAES Region

Croatian President Franjo Tudjman made a working visit to the UN-TAES Region on December 3rd. He met with Jacques and with local political leaders at UNTAES Headquarters. After seeing Vukovar he visited Djeletovci, Nijemci and drove through the southern portion of the Region to Lipovac. President Tudjman's discussions here with political leaders were a continuation of important political dialog, which had included a series of talks with Croatian Government officials. The local Executive Council also met with President Tudjman in Zagreb on November 9th.

Human Rights and Elections

These discussions emphasized the equal civil, human and personal rights of all citizens of Croatia of all ethnic backgrounds. Also discussed at the Vukovar meeting was the forthcoming free elections here, leading to comprehensive political representation at the national, regional and local levels. Also, a quicker and easier system for issuing documents to the thousands of people who are requesting them at several document offices in the Region was planned.

Reason and Dialogue

It was emphasized during the meeting that it is the task of reasonable people from both sides to engage in this political dialogue for the benefit of the population of the Region. Those who deny reality, who oppose dialogue and constructive solutions and who oppose the UN-TAES mandate of peaceful reintegration are really opposing and damaging the interests of the great majority of people of the Region who want to live here in peace and security.

UNTAES shuttle bus service Osijek-Beli Manister-Osijek

UNTAES Civil Affairs operated a shuttle bus service between Beli Manastir and Osijek. Anyone from Baranja with a Croatian ID could submit a request for a seat on the bus with the UNTAES Civil Affairs Office in Beli Manastir.

The bus left from outside the Belbat compound in Beli Manastir at 0700 hours and returned from Osijek at 1800 hours. A person may stay for more than one day in Osijek; however, he/she needed to inform the Civil Affairs Office of the date of return. The other bus service from Osijek to Beli Manastir, which started on 21 November, differed in that for the time being, passengers had to return on the same day. It left at 1000 hours from the abandoned INA station near Bilje and returned to the same point at 1900 hours. Those who wished to travel on this bus could book it at the UNTAES Osijek Office.

UN bus ready to depart from Osijek

Only 21 passengers could be booked each way and people were notified one day in advance of their departure. The buses operated Monday - Friday.

Use of Kuna in the Region

During December, the Kuna came into increasing use throughout the Region and many salaries were paid in Kuna as appropriate banking exchange offices were established. The Kuna then circulated freely here along with the Dinar, Dutche Mark and US dollar.

Transitional Schools

Beginning on December 2nd, six Hungarian schools in the Baranja introduced the Croatian Curriculum designed for the Hungarian minority in Croatia. The schools, in Zmajevac, Suza, Kotlina, Lug, Vardarac and Kopacevo, were called Transitional Schools. Earlier, the Joint Implementation Committee (JIC) on Education and Culture had coordinated the training of teachers from these schools.

Document Offices

Two more offices for the issuance of Croatian documents opened in the Region on December 3rd in Markusica and Sidski Banovci. Both offices were co-located with the local records offices.

Missing Persons

The former United States Secretary of State, Cyrus Vance, Chairman of the International Commission on Missing Persons (ICMP) in former Yugoslavia, visited UNTAES HQ to meet with Jacques and with representatives of both Serb and Croatian organizations concerned with missing persons. He was accompanied by Mr. Cornelio Sommaruga, President of the International Committee of the Red Cross, Mr. Jose Ayala Lasso, UN High Commissioner for Human Rights and Mr. Max van der Stol, OSCE High Commissioner on National Minorities. The visit to Vukovar formed part of a larger program of visits to Zagreb, Belgrade, Sarajevo and Pale.

ICMP delegation meets with local organizations

Transitional Customs Service

A Transitional Customs and Immigration Service (TCS) was inaugurated at the Erdut bridge on December 3rd. Based on the model of the Transitional Police Force (TPF), the TCS operated under the direction of Jacques with both Serb and Croatian customs officers. Customs revenues remained in the Region as part of the local government budget. The TCS operated on all international borders of the Region. The TCS operation did not affect the cross-border movement of people.

Displaced persons and refugees

UN High Commissioner for Refugees (UNHCR) was the lead agency responsible for the return of displaced persons to and from the Region. UNHCR was able to help displaced persons who required limited assistance in returning to their homes. Both agencies collaborated to identify displaced persons who wished to return and be reunited with their families or have a home that was in livable condition. If you met this criteria, contact one of the UNTAES Civil Affairs Offices listed below. The process took time, and you had to be in possession of your Domovnica and Croatian Identification Card (ID) before returning to your home. UNTAES Civil Affairs Officers, who specialized in displaced person issues, were available to meet with people and provide assistance with the following ground rules:

1. Advice on the procedures regarding a return; 2. Assist in the processing of requests for documents in the UNTAES Document Centers and ensure that the request was handled as quickly as possible; and 3. Consult with UNHCR and local officials in the area to which one wanted to return.

UNHCR was notified of the return and met people upon their arrival or soon afterwards, to monitor the return and assist them if they were experiencing any difficulties

UNHCR Protection Officers were located throughout Croatia to assist with returns.

Election Planning for the Region

The joint implementation committee (JIC) on elections, which involved local Serb and Croatian Government representation, continued its work planning for elections in the spring.

UNTAES supervised the elections in the Region, which were held in accordance with the highest international standards. The JIC transformed itself into a provisional electoral commission with the authority to ensure that the elections were held properly.

Important areas of agreement mainly concerned procedural issues such as setting up voting stations, preparing and storing of ballot papers and the counting of votes. The election date and requirements for voter eligibility were discussed by the JIC and Jacques made the final decision on those issues in accordance with his authority under the Security Council resolution. In connection with elections, additional offices were opened to issue Croatian citizenship and other documents.

Donors' Meeting for Regional Assistance

UNTAES hosted the first Donors' Meeting for the Region in Zagreb on December 6th. Titled "The Challenge of Reconstruction", it continued fund raising for reconstruction projects in the Region. $37 million was pledged during the meeting and more was expected after participants further studied the numerous proposals. Chaired by UNTAES Deputy TA Derek Boothby, the meeting was attended by more than 240 representatives from embassies, international organizations and agencies, financial institutions and non-governmental organizations (NGOs). Representatives of the local Serb authority and the Croatian Government addressed the meeting.

Hosting the Donors

Experts identified more than 100 major project proposals needed for reconstruction, which covered infrastructure, buildings, de-mining, restoration of public services and transport. This also included a massive reconstruction program to replace more than 25,000 devastated houses. At the meeting, emphasis was placed on the initial phase of revitalization, which could be undertaken immediately.

Dr. Vojislav Stanimirovic, who led the 17-member delegation representing the local Serb authorities, said that priority should be given to improving sectors such as agriculture, industry, oil resources, water supply, transport, health and electricity. The Croatian Government delegation, which was led by Deputy Prime Minister and Minister of Development and Reconstruction, Prof. Jure Radic, focused on issues relating to the return of Croatian displaced persons, reconstruction of housing units, development of infrastructure, restoration of telecommunications, establishment of a railway network and de-mining. Prof. Radic reiterated the Croatian Government policy of granting loans to individuals, regardless of ethnicity, to facilitate the rebuilding or repairing of their houses.

The pledges and commitments amounting to about $37 million came from the European Commission-$10 million; United States Agency for

International Development-$16 million as long-term assistance up to 1998 and $2 million for short-term technical assistance; Germany-$3.5 million; ltaly-$3 million; Belgium-$2 million; France- $500,000; The Netherlands-$180,000 and United Kingdom-$120,000.

Besides these pledges, the World Bank provided a loan for the reconstruction process in the Region. While most of the donations were made for general projects, some donors picked specific projects aimed at humanitarian assistance. Many donors indicated they would be taking the project proposals to their national capitals and would make their pledges after the projects were studied in detail. Mr. Boothby said he hoped these pledges would be the start of much larger funding for the Region in the years to come. Dr. Stanimirovic said that the first pledges indicated the commitment of the international community for a long-term engagement in the Region. A follow-up to the Donors' Meeting was planned to take place in about eight weeks.

Answers to some common questions about Croatian Documents

UNTAES received many inquiries concerning Croatian documents. Here we answered some common questions.

What is a Domovnica?

A Domovnica is a government issued document that certifies you are a Croatian citizen. It is essential to have a Domovnica in order to apply for other important Croatian Government documents.

Why is Citizenship Needed?

Under current Croatian law, citizenship is a requirement for guaranteeing certain rights, for example;

Selling your land, your house, or other real property located in Croatia;

Obtaining a pension from the Croatian Government;

Obtaining a Croatian ID card and/or passport,

Education and health benefits…voting and being elected to office;

Obtaining property compensation,. and

Obtaining reconstruction assistance.

Can I obtain Croatian Documents at a Documents Center even if I am originally from another area of Croatia?

Yes, you can obtain a Domovnica and other Croatian documents even though you are a displaced person from another part of Croatia where you had a legal domicile and you are entitled to Croatian citizenship.

What Documents should I take with me to obtain Domovnica and can I keep them?

Domovnica can be issued on the basis of Croatian Government records. You should take personal identification documents such as an old Yugoslav passport, old Croatian ID card, birth certificate, or local ID card. You are entitled to keep all documents, which you must show at the Documents Center, to prove your identity when you apply for a Domovnica.

Must I go to the Document Center in person?

Yes. Anyone who wants to obtain Croatian Government documents must go in person to a Documents Center to request and receive their documents.

What if my request for Domovnica is denied? Is there anything I can do?

Yes, if your request is denied, it is possible to pursue the issue further and attempt to obtain a positive decision by appealing to the Administrative Court. The Civil Rights Project can assist you with such an appeal. If you have more questions, you can contact the UNTAES Civil Affairs office. Or contact the Civil Rights Project.

Can I apply for all documents at one time?

Under the present Croatian system at the UDCs, you must first apply for a Domovnica. You can also apply for a birth certificate at the same time if you need one. After you receive your Domovnica, you can apply for an identity card. After you receive your ID card, you can apply for a passport.

How long does it take for my documents to be completed?

The time can vary depending on the case.

How do I know if my Domovnica and other documents are completed and ready to be collected from the UDC?

Currently there are seven UNTAES Document Centers (UDCs), where Croatian officials will issue your Domovnica as well as other Croatian Government documents, such as birth certificates, ID cards and passports. Staff members from UNTAES Civil Affairs are present in each office.

Can a Domovnica be denied?

No. Requests for persons listed in the citizenship records cannot be denied. Anyone listed in the citizenship records is automatically entitled to a Domovnica.

What if I do not have any Personal Identity Documents?

Even if you do not have personal identity documents, you are still entitled to request Domovnica at the UDCs, but the process of checking to establish your eligibility may take longer.

What if the records in my Place of Birth have been destroyed, can I still obtain Domovnica?

Yes, but there will be a different process, which will probably take somewhat longer. After you apply for a Domovnica, if the citizenship records from your place of birth have been destroyed, you will receive a document indicating that fact. If you receive such a document, you can still request Domovnica by applying to the Ministry of Interior officials at the UDC, to be rewritten in the citizenship records. In this case, it is useful to bring any and all documents, which establish your citizenship, such as a birth certificate, old Yugoslav passport, old Socialist Republic of Croatia ID card, etc.

If my documents are not ready, does that mean my request has been denied?

No. Requests for Domovnica and other documents can only properly be denied in writing. However, if it has been more than 60 days since you requested Domovnica and 15 days in the case of ID cards, you should inquire about the reason for the delay through a special form issued for that purpose.

How do I know if my Domovnica and other Documents are completed and ready to be collected from the UDC?

Currently the only way to find out if your Croatian documents are finished is to check with the UDC, either in person or by phone. However, the Croatian authorities are now preparing notices about those documents, which they have issued so that people can come and take them.

Since the opening of the first document center on 20 August, more than 20,000 people had applied for Domovnic's, out of which more than 18,000 had already received their citizenship papers. Several thousand other applications for birth certificates, ID cards and passports had also been processed.

CHAPTER 14

THE UNTAES MILITARY FORCE

Putting the UNTAES Military Force into place was not an easy task. What Jacques had to do in order to get the military forces needed for the mission, was to go to the different countries individually and ask for support. There is NO standing UN military force, which makes putting together any kind of military group quite a challenge. Of course, a lot of this has to do with money. If countries are strapped for cash, they are more interested in joining a UN Mission because their troops get paid by the UN. It was so difficult for the Russian troops that since they had no funds to pay their troops, they siphoned off gasoline from the UN tanks and sold it to the local Serbs on the open market. How about that for creativity?

The UN Security Council in its resolution 1079 established the UN-TAES mandate authorizing force strength of 5,000 troops for the mission. The then UN Secretary-General Boutros Boutros-Ghali appointed Major-General Jozef Schoups of Belgium as the first Force Commander.

General Schoups began planning for the mission immediately upon his appointment on January 15, 1996. On March 31st, the military headquarters became operational in Vukovar. Two battalions, Russian and Belgian, were already deployed to the region while battalions from

159

Jordan and Pakistan joined the mission on April 22nd. By May 5th, all military components were in place.

Support units such as the Ukrainian Helicopter and Tank Squadrons, Argentinean Reconnaissance Company, Slovakian Engineers and Indonesian and Czech medical units also took their positions.

On May 21st, the order for demilitarization was given and by June 20th, demilitarization was complete. UNTAES soldiers assumed responsibility for the Regions security.

As the Force Commander said, "...not a single life had been lost in military action. Not a de-miner, not a soldier, not an UNTAES civilian, nor a local Serb or Croat had been killed". This was a remarkable accomplishment in view of the results that had been achieved.

<u>Securing the Region for Peaceful Reintegration</u>

A U.N. observation post being manned around the clock

U.N. choppers fly in formation over the Drava River

Tanks on display and ready for action

A Message from the Transitional Administrator

Major General Klein reviews his troops at Klisa airfield

To My Fellow Soldiers

The UNTAES mission had remarkable success during 1996. One of the greatest accomplishments was the demilitarization of the Region, a task in which all of you played a very important part.

That accomplishment and the sense of security which your presence meant in the Region made it possible for us to carry out other tasks in safety. Peacekeeping is the true objective of all soldiers.

It is violence and war that is the enemy. Our goal is to save civilian lives and property and to provide security for a normal life. As we begin the New Year, it is fitting that we gather in your honor to express the immense respect and affection that you have earned from the people of the Region and from all of UNTAES. I am sure that your tour of duty in UNTAES has been a unique experience that will stand you in good stead wherever you go in the future. My best wishes will always be with you.

A Message from outgoing Force Commander Major-General Jozef Schoups

Major General Jozef Schoups talks to his troops

Dear Friends:

Your Force Commander is delighted to share a few thoughts with you. The occasion is very special indeed...the end of the first year of the UNTAES mandate, the end of 1996 and the end of my work here as Force Commander, your leader and adviser. All of you have done a great job; all of you are professional soldiers.

I would like to express my deep gratitude to all the Heads of States of the Troop Contributing Nations representing the International Force: Argentina, Belgium, the Czech Republic, Indonesia, Jordan, Pakistan, Poland, the Russian Federation, Slovakia and Ukraine, for making available such excellent soldiers for this mission. My experience in this Region was unique.

On January 15, 1997 I will leave you. I know that you will support my successor, Major General Willy Hanset, the way you have supported me. I hope that 1997 will bring peace and fulfillment of your wishes for you, your families, your friends and your loved ones. I wish you all the very best for the future.

<u>Russian Battalion</u>

In April 1992, the Russian Battalion with a total strength of 1,175 men (1 HQ company and 5 rifle companies) was deployed in Yugoslavia to Implement UN peacekeeping tasks in former Sector East.

The area of responsibility (AOR) of the battalion was approximately 1,500 square kilometers; the total length of the Zone of Separation (ZOS) was approximately 120 kilometers. The service was organized at 52 posts (5 checkpoints, 11 control posts, 4 crossings and 36 observation posts).

Since March 29, 1994 RUSBAT had performed tasks such as supporting the implementation of the Cease-fire Agreement in the ZOS, mediating conflicts and providing security for different organizations during negotiations. In May 1994, besides the ongoing implementation of the Cease-Fire Agreement, RUSBAT rendered assistance in withdrawal of weapons outside the 20 and 10 km zones (in accordance with the 29 March 94 Cease-fire Agreement). Continuing its deployment in the Region under the UNTAES mandate, RUSBAT played an important part in demilitarization. The battalion also provided security for de-mining teams in the following areas: the railway line between Vinkovci-Mirkovci; along the Drava river; in the villages of Antunovac and Divos and in other areas.

March past at a medals parade

Martial arts demonstration

In August 96, RUSBAT provided security during de-mining of the bridge next to the Osijek-Vukovar road and provided security for the Saturday open-air market place that was held near that bridge. The battalion also provided security during family reunion meetings at the Sarvas-Nemetin and Nustar-Brsadin crossing points. RUSBAT escorted convoys coming in to the Region with fertilizer, flour, wheat, reconstruction materials and other items and also provided security for various delegations coming to the Region.

In the humanitarian field, the RUSBAT medical unit provided primary and advanced medical assistance to countless numbers of local people who came to the facilities in Klisa and to mobile centers.

Belbat XIV

The arrival of Belgian peacekeepers to Baranja in April 1992, marked the start of the United Nations presence in the region. Since that date, 13 Belgian Battalions completed rotations in Baranja. The current battalion at that time, BELBAT XIV was made up of 618 soldiers and had begun its four-month tour of duty at the beginning of December. Its area of responsibility (AOR) was the northern part of the Baranja. It had two armored infantry companies, one reconnaissance support company from Argentina, one light reconnaissance company, one HQ Company, one combat engineering platoon, a radio transmission detachment, a de-mining detachment, a surgical team for quick intervention and a liaison team for air support.

The Belgian Battalion HQ was in Beli Manastir and the troops were stationed at the following locations: an armored infantry company in Baranjsko Petrovo Selo; an armored infantry company in Udvar; one platoon situated at the crossing of Batina; a light reconnaissance company in Branjin Vrh; a logistics company located in Beli Manastir and a combat engineering platoon located in Brod Pustara.

The reinforcement elements for the logistics, medical, communications and de-mining units of the land forces were located in Beli Manastir.

Belbat XIV carried on the practice established by its predecessors of high visibility and contact with the local population. One of the most important aspects of this was the medical assistance provided by Belbat doctors. They were sometimes the only source of medical care available to people, especially those in remote villages.

Like the other Battalions, Belbat also provided security and escort to visiting delegations and convoys bringing in goods to the Region.

A unique feature in Belbat was the transmission of their Radio Blue Sky. Started under Belbat VI in March 1994, it provided news, information and music to the Belgian troops relayed via satellite from Belgium.

Standing alert at an Operational site

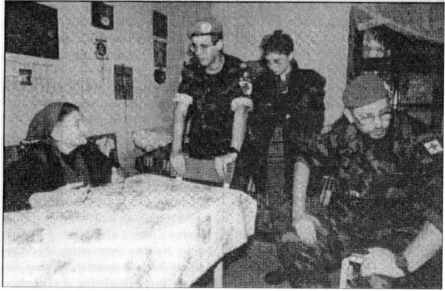

BELBAT doctors visiting the local population

Pakbat

Pakistan firmly believed in the principles of the United Nations charter and actively participated in UN missions. Pakistan contributed troops for 12 different UN peacekeeping missions besides hosting three UN Observer Groups in Pakistan. Forty-two men of the Pakistani Army laid down their lives while performing duties as UN peacekeepers. The Pakistani Contingent in UNTAES' (total 981) consisted of a Mechanized Infantry Battalion, an Armored Squadron, an Artillery Battery, an Engineers Platoon, a Signal Platoon, a Services Support Company, an Electrical and Mechanical Engineers Unit and a Medical Platoon.

Keeping in touch with HQ

Pakbat soldiers on a social patrol

The operational responsibility in the southern part of the Baranja was taken over from Belbat by the Pakistan Contingent on May 6, 1996

The main operational responsibilities were:

- Patrolling: Day and night patrolling in the AOR; an average of twenty patrols were sent out daily.

- Observation Posts: Prior to demilitarization Pakbat manned twelve OPs, six permanent and six temporary. They manned five OP's as the posts located in the demilitarized zone were removed.

- Security, Protection and Escorting: Security was provided to the weekly family meetings at the Bilje crossing organized by the Red Cross. Protection and escorts were provided to various delegations visiting the region for official meetings, village visitations, media coverage, pension disbursements, survey of civil infrastructure, etc.

- Monitoring De-mining Projects: Assistance was provided to de-mining projects.

- Humanitarian: Pakistani Army doctors emerged as the "Most Wanted" UN peacekeepers among the local population in the Baranja Region. They treated over 5,000 civilian patients, including 226 surgical cases held in a makeshift hospital in Darda. Army doctors also accompanied troops on routine patrolling in far-flung areas carrying essential food supplies and medicines.

Jorbat

The Kingdom of Jordan highly valued the role of the United Nations. Having played an important role in the Middle-East peace process, Jordanian forces, under His Majesty King Hussein, were pleased to serve under the UN flag. Jordan's contributions to UN peacekeeping operations began in 1991, initially with one battalion deployed in the former Sector North in Croatia under the UNPROFOR mandate. The Jordanians came in for praise due to the high level of discipline and neutrality, which their battalions displayed. As a result, the UN requested more Jordanian troops to serve in UN missions. At one time there were three battalions serving in Croatia and a Jordanian General led UNPROFOR.

In the UNTAES Region the 865-strong Jordanian Battalion (Jorbat-4) deployed in April and based its headquarters in Djeletovci. Its area of responsibility (AOR) stretched across 615 square kilometers of the southern part of the UNTAES Region. Jorbat had two mechanized infantry companies located at Mirkovci and Nijemci.

Pakbat soldiers on social patrol

Jorbat played an important role in taking over the Djeletovci oil fields from local paramilitary forces, in securing the demilitarization of the Region, in opening of the Belgrade--Zagreb Highway at Lipovac and in facilitating the opening up of the Lipovac Corridor to unrestricted Croatian access. In addition to the traditional duties of monitoring checkpoints and patrolling in its AOR, Jorbat carried out social patrols in villages to establish direct contact with local people and to distribute humanitarian aid and provide medical assistance. Jorbat also facilitated the collection, storage and destruction of weapons, under the UNTAES "Buy-Back" program.

Slovak Engineering Battalion

This is the first military unit in the history of the army of the Slovak Republic, ever sent abroad on a UN peacekeeping mission. On May 1, 1993 the first train with the accommodation unit set out on a long journey from Slovakia to the former Yugoslavia. 409 soldiers arrived in Lipik in Western Slavonia in 9 trains, bringing with them all necessary engineering equipment and materials. Since then, Slovengbat has participated in peacekeeping missions under UNPROFOR, UNPF and UNTAES. In the UNTAES mission Slovengbat has 563 members consisting of a logistics support company, a field company and a heavy equipment company.

Mine clearing tank with rollers

Digging out a mine

A remote control operated de-mining vehicle is among the specialized pieces of de-mining equipment used in the mission. Since their deployment, Slovengbat has carried out an impressive number of tasks including:

- building 35 bridges

- repairing and maintaining 510 km of roads

- demining an area of 2 million square meters

- defusing 2,000 pieces of ammunition

Additionally, the construction platoon built a number of new camps for UNTAES contingents, including kitchens and accommodation areas.

Indonesian Medical Company

The Indonesian Medical Company (Indomedcoy) deployed to UNTAES on March 15, 1996 and was located in Erdut.

Indomedcoy provided medical assistance to UNTAES civilian and military personnel in the mission area. The Company was made up of 72 personnel including a General Surgeon, Digestive Surgeon, Orthopedics Surgeon, Oral Surgeon, Anesthetist, Internist, Neurologist, Dermatologist, Ear Nose and Throat specialist, Psychiatrist, seven General Practitioners" two Dentists, Radiographer, Laboratory Analyst and Paramedics. The Company was equipped with six ambulances and four Rapid Ambulance Teams.

Indomedcoy treated more than 12,000 patients, 10,000 of which were local residents. Indomedcoy also provided medical support in demining operations, family reunions, village visitations, VIP escorts, the weekly open-air market in Klisa, Osijek, and was also stationed at the Lipovac highway.

The Company provided Hygiene and Sanitation Control for all UNTAES Units including Environment Sanitation Control, Food control, Water Sources Control and Pest control. Indomedcoy collaborated and coordinated with WHO, UNHCR and other NGOs, for the distribution of medical supplies to various local clinics in the Region.

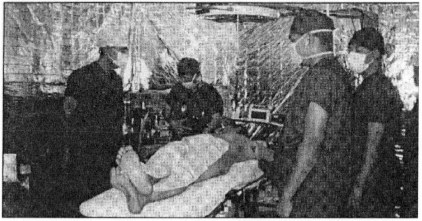

Preparing for surgery

The Polish Special Police Group

The Polish company consisted of 53 soldiers and arrived in the Region in December. It **wa**s a quick reaction force, whose main task was to perform security assistance tasks where required. It is also geared to provide escort for official visitors.

UN Military Observers

United Nations Military Observers (UNMOs), with a nearly 50-year history of being deployed in many peacekeeping missions, made important contributions to the successful demilitarization of the UN-TAES Region. Essential to carrying out this task was the close coordination with the liaison officers of both sides.

There were about 100 UNMOs, ranking from Captains to a Brigadier-General, from 23 different countries. The breadth of experience and the multinational composition ensured that each team was unbiased and capable of handling a multitude of situations. They brought with them the specialized skills and knowledge gained through experience.

Checking out community needs

Living and working in the community, the UNMOs operated an open door policy, cooperating with local authorities and local people. They answered questions, offered advice and directed visitors to the UN agency best able to deal with their specific problems.

Argentine Reconnaissance Company

The Argentine Reconnaissance Company deployed in UNTAES was the first unit from Argentina that was under the operational control of a foreign military command. Based in Brod Pustara in the Baranja, the Argentine Recce Coy functions under the command of the Belgian Battalion in Beli Manastir.

Led by Major Raul Galla, the 74 men strong Argentinean Reconnaissance Company had four combat platoons consisting of two tank platoons and two mechanized infantry platoons equipped with armored personnel carriers (APCs). A reserve platoon was always on stand-by. Since its deployment in May 96, the Recce Coy carried out 24-hour patrols in its area of responsibility. It also operated mobile checkpoints and an observation post.

Ukrainian Helicopter Squadron

The Ukrainian Helicopter Squadron (Heli Sqn) deployed to UNTAES with a 239-strong contingent based in Klisa. It contained six MI-24 attack Helicopters and six MI -8 transport helicopters.

U.N. Helicopter Squadron chopper used to transport personnel and cargo

The Heli Squadron played an important role in the demilitarization of the UNTAES Region by providing air reconnaissance and air patrolling. Another important task was providing transportation to UN personnel and cargo and carrying out medical evacuations.

Ukranian Light Infantry Company

The Ukrainian light Infantry Company replaced the tank squadron, which rotated out of the mission in November. Based in Marinovci, the infantry Coy was established to provide support for special projects.

Czech Field and Surgical Hospital

The Czech field hospital was relocated from Pleso in Zagreb to Klisa in the UNTAES mission area in March 96. With a staff strength of 38, including specialist doctors, surgeons, nurses and paramedics, and a well-equipped operating theater. The field hospital was geared to provide routine, as well as emergency medical services.

Medics check troops in the field

Jacques was trying to motivate people in the Region to think about what was taking place, to understand that things were changing and that they needed to become engaged in the process. This message was an attempt to do just that. The people had to take responsibility for their future and not be afraid to get out and vote when the time came. Here he talks about the great accomplishments of the UNTAES Mission and encourages the people to emotionally move forward.

MESSAGE TO THE PEOPLE OF THE REGION FROM THE TRANSITIONAL ADMINISTRATOR

Residents of the UNTAES Region, citizens of Croatia, my friends:

These are critical and historic days for each and every one of you. This week the Security Council will study and approve the recent Letter of the Croatian Government, which gives specific guarantees to you based on the Erdut Agreement. It is now up to each of you to make your own choice.

That choice is either to work towards a safe, dignified and prosperous future by taking your rights as Croatian citizens, or to cross the river back to the past and live an uncertain and impoverished life as exiles in somebody else's land.

You have come to where you are today through a brutal and painful conflict fueled from outside this Region but resulting in war and destruction here. You have suffered from somebody else's ambitions. It was a grand delusion, with tragic consequences and you have paid the price.

For five years the war and cease fires dragged on. You became more and more impoverished, and the balance of military power shifted. Every peace plan, every constructive initiative put forward by the international community, was rejected by false leaders. It was only the international community that prevented further war here which surely would have resulted in death, destruction and further flight.

Basic Agreement

The signing of the Basic Agreement on November 12, 1995, gave you a chance, which became a hope, when the Security Council established UNTAES with the goal of peacefully reintegrating this Region and its residents into the Republic of Croatia.

You all know what we have done since last spring. The Region is demilitarized. Communications and transportation links are restored and roads, railways, telephone services and waterways are open. We have reintegrated public enterprises and secured permanent jobs for employees who work there. Over 130,000 people have met at the weekly UNTAES market and used the sponsorship and other programs designed to help people reunite.

We have implemented more than 50 quick-impact economic projects, and raised pledges of over $37 million dollars to revive the catastrophic economic situation in the Region.

Last week, distribution of pensions began to 22,000 residents of the Region. I hope you will agree with me that the future is in your hands.

CHAPTER 15

JACQUES APPEALS TO THE POPULACE

Jacques appealed to the public, using children as a backdrop in the photo below, to help motivate the parents of the next generation. Our goal was to make sure people understood the changes that were taking place and that their future was in their own hands. This was a difficult concept for people to grasp, having been raised in a controlled Eastern European environment. It was terrifying for them, especially realizing that UNTAES would eventually leave and that the terror might begin again.

Jacques stands in the midst of the children of Ilok.

What you must do now

We had reached a point in time where there was less for UNTAES to do and more for the people to do. The responsibility had shifted to the people and the Croatian Government to take the future into their own hands. UNTAES could not help them unless they helped themselves.

The Letter on the Completion of Reintegration of the Region held promise for a secure future, and the elections were their opportunity to seize that future. The Letter was not just the result of the efforts of UNTAES, it was also the result of their efforts and particularly the views of the thousands of ordinary people who had come to Jacques, in churches, in factories, at town meetings and on farms to express their hopes for a better future.

Consultation

The idea that the Letter was drafted without consultation with the local leadership was nonsense. Since early August, the Serb leadership has been meeting with all levels of the Croatian Government, including President Tudjman in Zagreb and Vukovar, to state their concerns. When President Tudjman met with Serb leaders in Vukovar in November, it came as a surprise to many people. But we were heartened by the comment of one Serb who said: "If President Tudjman can come to Vukovar, maybe I don't need to leave."

For three months, negotiations on elections were paralyzed by the insistence of the Regional assembly on a single Zupanija. This demand had no support from the international community and no basis in the Erdut Agreement. A single Zupanija did not exist before the war and the creation of a single Zupanija after would be an invitation to division rather than unity.

We decided to make one final effort to produce the best possible political package, which would guarantee the Serb and other ethnic communities in the Region a safe, dignified and prosperous future. Even though the Regional assembly rejected further negotiations, on December 26th, Jacques wrote to President Tudjman outlining possible elements of a comprehensive political package. At the same time, he wrote to Dr. Stanimirovic asking him and the Executive Council to show true leadership and move forward. President Tudjman responded positively to his proposals. Dr. Stanimirovic, for political reasons, was unable to do the same. For the next two weeks, UNTAES worked hard to improve the document and what UNTAES did achieve were proposals, which met the highest of international standards.

<u>What you get</u>

There were three general issues. What you got from elections, what you got regardless of election results, and what you got as broad guarantees.

For elections, everyone who was eligible for Croatian citizenship and who lived in the Region before January 15, 1996, could vote. Displaced persons who arrived after 1991 could choose to vote in Vukovar or for elections in their original home areas.

The local Serb community could appoint a Joint Council of Municipalities, which would meet with the President or his Chief of Staff at least every 4 months. Regardless of election results, the Serb community would have a Deputy Zupan post in each of the two Zypanijas, Assistant Minister positions at the Ministries of Interior, Justice, Education and Culture; and senior positions in the Ministry of Reconstruction and Development and the Office for Displaced Persons and Refugees. These were important positions of authority, providing real access to power. Two Serbs from the Region were to be appointed to the Upper House of the Sabor, and after the next census, Serbs would have proportional representation in the House of Representatives. In addition, the Serb community throughout Croatia would be able to form a Council of the Serb Ethnic Community, which would be a vote to promote the interests of all Serbs in Croatia.

The Letter also spelled out specific guarantees including educational and cultural autonomy. War victims would have full health and social rights. Compulsory military service would be deferred for 2 years after which further deferment would be possible upon personal application. And above all, these were international commitments by Croatia, for which the international community would hold it accountable. These commitments elaborated and went far beyond the minimum requirements of the Basic Agreement.

Challenge and choice

The challenge and choice was now up to them. UNTAES recommended they not follow those extremists who wanted the public to refuse their rightful citizenship documents, who would deny their right to vote and who would lead them once again into exile. The essence of democracy was for citizens to stand up for their rights. For them, the challenge was to take their citizenship, organize themselves into political parties, exercise their right to vote, and take up the full rights and obligations of the Croatian constitution and law.

UNTAES had essentially completed its political tasks. UNTAES had built on the structure of the Basic Agreement and ensured that they had a comprehensive set of guarantees for their future life in Croatia. We created the conditions under which they could freely exercise their democratic right to stay or to leave. But, if they chose to leave, they did so as economic migrants, of their own free choice, heading for an uncertain future in troubled lands. It was time for all the local leadership, which claimed to represent their interests, to have the vision and wisdom to put personal biases aside and truly represent their interests.

For many months Jacques fought with them to enable pensioners to receive their pensions, to integrate companies so that jobs were guaranteed and fair wages paid and to engage cooperatively in giving the residents of the Region a real future.

The reasons for delay and obstruction had not been because of the will of the majority but because of the misconceptions and material self-interest of a few.

It was time for them to see the light as well. It was time to reject the past and failed policies that had brought the people to this point. If they could not do this, then they should leave and let the decent people of the Region, get on with their lives.

Displaced persons

Finally, Jacques had a special message for the displaced persons…Serbs, Croats and other ethnic groups. They were the special victims of this war. Every one of them had the right to go home. No one wished to live in someone else's house. This was a year of return and reconciliation. But they could not do it on their own and they could not do it if they continued to oppose one another. Money was desperately required for reconstruction of homes and de-mining of the land. At least $1 billion was required. This was beyond the resources of Croatia alone. International assistance was essential to quicken the pace of return and ensure that when they went home, they could do so safely and not lose an arm or a leg to a mine explosion. The one sure way to get international assistance was to work together and to jointly appeal for help. Displaced persons were all victims of this war. Only by working together and setting up a single organization, would they be able to more quickly and safely rebuild their lives in their real homes.

The choice was theirs to make

The choice belonged to the people. One path led to a future with dignity and security in the land where their ancestors had lived for centuries and where their homes, churches and traditions were. This path gave a future to their children and the ability for the people to reunite with their families and friends. It was a path fully supported by the international community and that community agreed to do all in its power to help them achieve their goals.

The other path led to uncertain exile in troubled lands, where little awaited them except the strong likelihood that they would one day deeply regret their decision.

While they could not forget the past, they also could not change it. But, if they worked together, they could shape and structure a better future.

Pensioners receive advance payment and get documents

The Croatian Government in cooperation with UNTAES carried out a program under which it made a one-time payment of 500 Kuna to people in the Region who were receiving pensions in 1991. This payment was an advance on future compensations from the Croatian pension system. For these pensioners, preprinted Domovnicas would be available at the same time and Croatian ID cards also would be prepared on site. Taking the Domovnica and I.D card was not a precondition for receiving the pension amount.

The packet for each pensioner included on the pension lists for the Region before October 8, 1991 included: a 500 Kuna payment in small bills; an ID card which had to be signed, as well as photographed, fingerprinted and laminated and an application for enrollment into the Croatian pension system to be mailed to the appropriate office.

The pension payments and documents were being distributed directly by Croatian officials, with UNTAES coordinating the program and providing security. There were 4 stationary teams in Beli Manastir, Darda, Borovo Naselje, and Vukovar.

An additional 7 mobile teams traveled through the Region, making payments in each town out of predetermined sites--usually local offices, schools, or registry offices. Over 4,000 such payments were made. Pensioners who had moved to the Region from other parts of Croatia received their pensions in the second phase of the program. UNTAES and the Croatian authorities worked with the local pension fund and the Croatian pension fund to prepare a list of pre-1991 pensioners from other parts of Croatia.

CHAPTER 16

CROATIA CONTACTS SECURITY COUNCIL

At an early point in the Mission, Jacques asked me to go with him to a luncheon at President Tudjman's palace in Zagreb. The palace was beautiful, the food was great and the service was outstanding. There was chitchat with foreign representatives and a few of Croatia's leaders. Unfortunately, President Tudjman did not attend. However, toward the end of the Mission, I did meet President Tudjman. He flew in unannounced from Zagreb one afternoon to the Vukovar compound where we had established our headquarters. Even though he had good protection surrounding him, he appeared to be extremely nervous. I guess that's understandable, considering he was right in the middle of "enemy country".

Executive Council representatives with President Tudjman and Jacques at UNTAES HQ

The Croatian Government submitted a Letter to the UN Security Council on January 13th outlining a number of measures, which it would take to ensure full political representation, voting rights, educational and cultural autonomy and other rights for the population of the Region.

The Letter came about as a result of a long series of consultations. Jacques took the Regional Serb Executive Council to Zagreb twice. We had Croatian Government Ministers from Zagreb in Vukovar. These matters were discussed between local political leaders and President Tudjman during meetings both in Zagreb and in Vukovar. And there had been an enormous amount of discussion of the details in order to come up with the most comprehensive package possible. First, it was decided to have an election simultaneous with nationwide elections, which were scheduled for March 16, 1997. Every citizen of Croatia who lived in the Region as of January 15, 1996 could vote. It would be their first time to really articulate their political will. This guaranteed clear cultural and religious and educational autonomy, representation in the upper and lower house, a minimum of 700-800 police in the Region from Serb and other ethnic minorities, specific positions in key Ministries in Zagreb, such as Interior, Justice, Education and Culture, Reconstruction and Development. It allowed for a Council of the Serb Ethnic Community, which had the right to appeal directly to the President on issues of common concern to the national minority. This was in addition to the Joint Council of Municipalities. It had a draft deferment and guaranteed Deputy Zupan positions. In other words, it was far beyond what the Erdut Agreement called for. In consultations with the Croatian Government, UNTAES had been very specific that the local population be represented and work in local education and health care organizations and the judiciary. In a message to the people of the Region Jacques solicited support for this. He explained that it would give people the kind of protection that would allow them to live with dignity and honor, and protect their rights and property. It was a major step towards reconciliation. The election allowed people to express their political will in terms of the leadership they wanted. Then the people could move forward to bring the process of peaceful reintegration to its conclusion.

Main Points of the Croatian Government Letter

- Elections in the Region concurrent with other Croatian voting were scheduled for mid-March

- All persons eligible for Croatian citizenship and in the Region as of January 15, 1996 (beginning of the UNTAES mandate) could vote.

- All voters were required to have Croatian documents

- Local Serb ethnic community had full political representation including Deputy Zupan in each Zupanija

- Proportional representation in local health, police and judicary services (including senior positions)

- During first year local police force would include and other non-Croat ethnic members

- There would be a Serb Joint Council of Municipalities

- Two representatives of the Serb Community would be appointed as deputies in the House of Counties

- Representatives of the local Serb community would be appointed to senior posts in the following: Ministry of Reconstruction and Development; Office of Displaced Persons and Refugees; Ministries: Interior, Justice, Education & Culture (Assistant Minister Level)

- Full rights for educational and cultural autonomy

- Council of Serb Ethnic Community (nationwide) promoted interest in the nation

- Deferment of requirement for military service for two years. (Further deferment possible upon application)

- Residents of the Region who were war victims (disabled, widows, orphans, etc.) had full health and social rights (except veteran's benefits) under "Rights of Croatian Defenders" law

- Points in this letter were additional earlier agreements/laws (Constitution, Basic Agreement, SC Resolution, Affidavit of Employment, etc)

LETTER BY THE GOVERNMENT OF THE REPUBLIC OF CROATIA ON THE COMPLETION OF PEACEFUL REINTEGRATION OF THE REGION UNDER THE TRANSITIONAL ADMINISTRATION, REPUBLIC OF CROATIA

Elections in the Region under the Transitional Administration were to be held pursuant to the Basic Agreement of 12 November 1995, under authority of the Transitional Administrator, and according to pro-es defined in the laws of the Republic of Croatia, on March 16.

The Government of Croatia provided full opportunity to all persons eligible to vote in elections for local bodies of authority in the region who appeared correctly on the voter lists for the elections. Elections for local bodies of authority in other areas of the Republic of Croatia were to be held on the same date.

Local bodies of authority, in parts of the Osijek-Baranja and Vukovar-Srijem Counties, which were under the Transitional Administration, were established, in accordance with the electoral results certified by the Transitional Administrator, and pursuant to the Constitution and laws of the Republic of Croatia, within the lawfully prescribed term but no later than 30 days after the elections.

Members of the local Serb ethnic community, as well as all other Croatian citizens were eligible for local elections if they were resident at the time of the 1991 census, in parts of Osijek-Baranja and Vukovar-Srijem Counties currently under the Transitional Administration. Possession of Croatian citizenship/identity documents was an essential prerequisite for participation in the elections.

Pursuant to the Basic Agreement of 12 November 1995, Croatian citizens who were members of the Serb ethnic community, settled into the area prior to the beginning of the UNTAES mandate and were currently living in the area under the Transitional Administration, that were not domiciled in that particular area at the time of the 1991 census, could choose to vote either for a) local bodies of authority established according to Croatian laws, provided that they were currently living in the areas covered by these bodies, whether the territory of these bodies was wholly or partially within such areas:, or b) such local bodies of authorities formed under Croatian laws, in the area of their 1991 residence.

In order to obtain a register of those Serbs who were not residents of the area at the time of the 1991 census, and who were currently living in the territory under UNTAES control, registration had to be organized by the Croatian authorities and UNTAES. Croatian authorities were required to issue citizenship / identity documents to those persons in sufficient time to enable them to participate in elections.

The Serb ethnic community from the area under the Transitional Administration was guaranteed to be represented in the bodies of local government and self -government pursuant to the rights and principles laid down in the Constitutional Law on the rights of ethnic Communities and National Minorities, and the Law on Local Government and Self-Government. It was guaranteed that they hold the post of Sub-Prefect in both Counties. Proportional Serb representation, including senior positions, in the local health services, police and judiciary in the area, now constituting the Region under the Transitional Administration, was guaranteed regardless of what administrative divisions were introduced in the future. For at least the first year following local elections, the number of local police from the Serb and other non-Croat ethnic communities would be approximately 700 to 800.

Members of the Serb ethnic community from the area under the Transitional Administration should appoint Joint Council of Municipalities. The leadership of the Joint Council of Municipalities should meet at least once every four months directly with the President of the Republic or with the chief of the Presidential cabinet.

Following the next census of the population of the inhabitants of the Republic of Croatia, the number of seats reserved at subsequent elections for members of the Serb and other national minorities in the House of Representatives of the Parliament of the Republic of Croatia, should reflect the proportion of their representation as determined by the census results.

With respect to representation in the House of Counties, the President of the Republic should appoint, pursuant to provision of Article 71, Paragraph 4 of the Constitution, two representatives from the Serb ethnic community as deputies in the House of Counties.

The representatives of the Serb ethnic community from the area under consideration were to be appointed to senior posts in the Ministry of

Reconstruction and Development, and Office for Displaced Persons and Refugees and at the level no lower than Assistant Minister in the Ministries of Interior, Justice, Education and Culture. In accordance with the laws and regulations of the Republic of Croatia, they were also to be entitled to appropriate participation at the expert level in the working bodies of the Parliament of the Republic of Croatia.

The Government of Croatia, in accordance with existing Croatian laws and statutes and internationally accepted standards, guaranteed that the members of the Serb minority, and other members of other minorities within the area under the Transitional Administration, had full rights with respect to educational and cultural autonomy.

With respect to education, the members of the Serb minority and the members of other minorities within the area under the Transitional Administration were entitled to prepare and implement curriculum, which fostered cultural identity, history and heritage in so far as it did not prejudicially affect any right or privilege with respect to international educational standards and Croatian laws.

The members of the Serb ethnic community were allowed to found the Council of the Serb Ethnic Community. The council was able to apply to the president of the Republic and the Croatian Government proposing and promoting the solution of issues of common interest for the national minority.

The Defense Minister was allowed to enact a special decision for all the members of the Serb ethnic community from the area under the Transitional Administration on the deferment of military service for a period of two years from the end of the UNTAES mandate. After the expiration of the two-year deferment period, the Ministry of Defense agreed to consider applications for deferment of military service at the personal request of the members of the Serb ethnic community in the area under Transitional Administration. Exemptions specified above were not limited in any way to the relevant civic rights of those concerned, including the right to obtain a Croatian passport, which was guaranteed to all citizens of Croatia by the Constitution.

Members of the Serb and other ethnic communities from the area under the Transitional Administration who were war victims, particularly disabled, widows and children without parents, had full health and social rights in accordance with the laws and regulations of the Republic of Croatia, except for the rights defined by the Law on Rights of Croatian Defenders.

The Government of the Republic of Croatia reaffirmed in this Letter of Intent, its commitments deriving from provisions of the Constitution of the Republic of Croatia, the Constitution Law on Human Rights and Freedom and the Rights of National and Ethnic Communities or Minorities in the Republic of Croatia, all other relevant laws, the Basic Agreement of November 1995, UN Security Council.

New Force Commander Takes UNTAES Command

General Willy Hanset receiving the UN Flag at the Transfer of Authority ceremony

Exactly a year after his appointment as UNTAES Force Commander, Major- General Jozef Schoups relinquished command to Major-General Willy Hanset at an impressive ceremony at the Klisa air base on January 15, 1997. The new Force Commander, General Hanset, was born in Belgium on September 21, 1943. His military career began when he graduated from the Second Lieutenant's Preparatory Course in 1964. General Hanset served in various commands and locations until December 26, 1994 when he was promoted to the rank of Major General and appointed Commander of a Combat Support Division in Belgium.

CHAPTER 17

SECURITY COUNCIL SUPPORTS ELECTIONS

In a Presidential Statement, the UN Security Council emphasized the importance of elections in the Region and called on the Croatian Government to quickly issue the required citizenship and identity papers. A few days later the local Regional Assembly agreed with the need to hold elections and also condemned all acts of violence in the Region.

The Security Council statement noted the Croatian Government Letter, which guarantees local cultural and educational autonomy; local Serb representation at the local, regional and national government level; a two-year deferment of military service; strong local representation in the police force, the judiciary and other public services; and other rights and guarantees.

The amnesty law, the right to return to homes and property compensation was also emphasized. The local Regional Assembly called on all people to stay in the Region and to ignore rumors. In this connection, the Transitional Administrator said on local TV, there would be no change in the rules for entry and exit to the Region during the UNTAES mandate. The present system remained unchanged.

U.N. Security Council and Secretary-General Kofi Annan

UN Secretary-General, Kofi Annan, in a letter to the President of the Security Council, reviewed efforts by UNTAES to resolve outstanding policy issues required for holding elections in the Region. The Secretary-General said that following intensive discussions by the TA with the parties involved, the Croatian Government had sent a letter to the Security Council outlining various guarantees as part of the peaceful reintegration of the Region. In a Presidential Statement issued on January 31, the Security Council called upon both parties to cooperate in good faith with the Transitional Administration in Eastern Slavonia, Baranja and Western Sirmium to ensure the success of the process of reintegration.

Main Points

The Security Council:

-- Underlined the importance of the holding of elections, under UNTAES organization, in accordance with the Basic Agreement

-- Emphasized that Croatian authorities fulfill their obligations with respect to the completion of the issuance of citizenship and identity documents for all eligible voters

-- Underlined the need for full cooperation by the local Serbs; Encouraged Croatian authorities to maintain the demilitarized status of the Region

-- Reiterated the right of all refugees and displaced persons to return to their places of origin

-- Strongly encouraged the Government of Croatia to reaffirm its obligations under the provisions of the Croatian Constitution, Croatian law, and the Basic Agreement, to treat all its citizens equally regardless of their ethnicity

-- Stressed that the restoration of the multi-ethnic character of Eastern Slavonia was important to international efforts to maintain peace and stability in the region of former Yugoslavia as a whole

-- Encouraged the Croatian Government to promote goodwill and build confidence by fully implementing its Law on Amnesty

-- Welcomed the commitments by the Government of Croatia with regard to the establishment of a Joint Council of Municipalities, Council of the Serb ethnic community, and with respect to educational and cultural autonomy of the Serb population and other minorities in the Region and

-- Called upon the international community to fully support the process of reintegration

Human Rights Group Monitored Regional Elections

The Office for Democratic Institutions and Human Rights (ODIHR), an institution of the Organization of Security and Cooperation in Europe (OSCE) monitored the UNTAES supervised elections in the Region.

The OSCE High Commissioner made the announcement for ethnic minorities, Max Van der Stoel, during his visit to UNTAES HQ in Vukovar on January 30th. Mr. Vander Stoel said that the OSCE was willing to send a sufficient number of monitors needed for the task. Mr. Vander Stoel appealed to the Serb population in the UNTAES Region not to leave. He expressed the hope that all those who had the right to vote would apply for a Domovnica and use their right to vote. Voters who did not go to the polls would fail to make use of the possibility to influence future decisions by casting their vote, he said. Mr. Van der Stoel said he was aware that there was a constant discussion among the Serb population of the Region about their security once Croatia re-established full administrative control on July 15th. He said that although UNTAES might end some of its tasks by July 15th, the UN would continue to stay on for another six months in a monitoring capacity. This monitoring was a very important guarantee for the Serb population, especially because this involved the implementation of the promises and assurances given by the Croatian Government to the community.

Max Van der Stoel

The Erdut agreement also made it quite clear that the Croatian Government would accept monitoring the respect of human rights by the international community on a long-term basis. Mr. Van der Stoel said that the OSCE had organized a conference the previous November with a number of other international organizations, such as the Council of Europe and the ECMM on how best to set up such a post-UNTAES monitoring system for future years. These consultations would intensify in the coming months and the key element of the discussions would be on how to make the monitoring as effective as possible. "This is not just a question of monitors moving around in jeeps, although that will no doubt be an important part of the exercise," Mr. Van der Stoel said. "What I am referring to is the assurance I received from the Croatian Government that it will cooperate with the long-term monitoring of the human rights in the Region, and also the promise that monitors would have freedom of movement and full access to all relevant information."

Mr. Van der Stoel said there was a long list of international treaties which Croatia had signed and which the Croatian Government had promised to apply completely in the present UNTAES area. He emphasized that various international organizations would take up the task of effective monitoring in the post-UNTAES period and check carefully that the Croatian Government kept its promises.

Ambassadors underline international support for peaceful reintegration

Diplomats in discussions with local leaders

199

A delegation of Zagreb-based Ambassadors and diplomats from the United States, Britain, France, Germany, Italy, the Russian Federation, Belgium, the Netherlands, Sweden, Norway, the Czech Republic, Slovakia, Ukraine and Spain visited the UNTAES Region on February 6th. The Ambassadors met with Jacques and senior UNTAES officials. Later, the group of Ambassadors met with the local Serb leadership. The Ambassadors emphasized that their countries supported the process towards elections and would ensure long-term international monitoring in the Region.

CHAPTER 18

ANSWERS TO PUBLIC QUESTIONS

We were attempting to do a modified "town hall meeting" and respond to some of the hundreds of questions that people had for UNTAES. Jacques was very good in a crowd and even though he couldn't understand exactly what the people were saying, he was able to physically interact with the populace...kind of like a political candidate would do in the U.S. He loved "pressing the flesh" and was right at home schmoozing with folks on the street or talking to politicians in the Region. It was an exciting time and in a strange, exhausting way, a great deal of fun.

A "Protectorate" for the Region for at least five years

The Basic Agreement provided that the maximum time period for the transitional period was two years, until January 15, 1998. The UN Security Council mandate for UNTAES was based upon the Basic Agreement. No "protectorate" was ever mentioned in the Basic Agreement. Successful implementation of the UNTAES mandate by the end of the transitional period meant that no "protectorate" was necessary. In part, it depended on active Serb political participation in the process of reintegration.

Recently there have been peaceful public demonstrations near UNTAES headquarters in Vukovar and elsewhere. Mr. Klein and other senior UN officials have met with several representatives from the groups involved to discuss their concerns. Here UNTAES responds to some of the questions which have been raised.

Jacques speaks with representatives of the demonstrators at UNTAES headquarters

Integrity of the Region

The Basic Agreement did not provide that the territory of the Region remain as a single electoral or administrative unit within Croatia. In fact, paragraph 12 of the Agreement specifically referred to "elections for all local government bodies, including municipalities, districts and counties"--all noted in the plural. This clearly indicated that the signatories to the Agreement were aware that the Region was not part of a single county or Zupanija. The demand for one Zupanija was unrealistic, as was recognized by the Security Council in its Presidential Statement.

Demilitarization of the Region Under the Basic Agreement

The Region was to remain demilitarized for the duration of the transitional period. The permanent demilitarization of the Region was something that was not under UNTAES control. The Presidential Statement of the Security Council encouraged the Croatian government to maintain the demilitarized status of the Region. Both Presidents Tudjman and Milosevic, with whom Jacques met, reacted positively to this idea.

Return of Displaced Persons

The return of displaced persons was not an issue over which UNTAES had responsibility. In cooperation with UNHCR, UNTAES worked on a whole program of reconstruction, compensation, and returns. The program addressed the issues of those who wanted to return home and alternatives for those who were not able to return to their original homes.

Right to vote for refugees and those who came to the Region after beginning of the UNTAES mandate

Paragraph 4 of the Basic Agreement, signed on November 12, 1995, guaranteed "all persons who left the Region or who had come to the Region with previous permanent residence in Croatia should enjoy the same rights as all other residents of the Region". The right to vote, among other rights, was thus guaranteed to all persons from Croatia who were in the Region by November 12, 1995. The Croatian Letter fulfilled that obligation and extended the date of residence up to January 15, 1996, the first day of the UNTAES mandate.

Amnesty for all Citizens

The Croatian Government told UNTAES that they would provide a comprehensive list of individuals who were subject to prosecution. Those not on the list would be covered by amnesty.

Military deferment

The Letter provided for a two-year deferment of military service from the end of the UNTAES mandate. Croatian officials, including Defense Minister Susak, also assured UNTAES that applications for a second period of three years for deferment of military service would be considered in a positive light. The Croatian army downsized from more than 200,000 to 60,000 personnel. It was expected to reduce further, as it planned for a smaller professional army.

Dual Citizenship

This was an issue outside of UNTAES' authority. We understood that Yugoslav law did not permit dual citizenship. Any agreement to permit dual citizenship would be a decision of the FRY Government based on bilateral discussions with the Croatian Government. However, we understood that the new FRY citizenship law provided that anyone who was a citizen of and resident in the former Yugoslavia on the date of adoption of the FRY Constitution could receive FRY citizenship within three years from the passage of the law. This provided a crucial guarantee until 1999. We expected the FRY government to reaffirm this fact.

Further Job Guarantees

The Government of Croatia issued an affidavit on December 16, 1996, whereby it agreed that the rights of employees of public enterprises and institutions would be protected in accordance with the legislation of the Republic of Croatia and with the relevant international standards, including those of the International Labor Organization. UNTAES secured additional guarantees for workers in the Region. After negotiations with the Croatian Government, employees of public enterprises and institutions had guarantees which included the following: the years of service from 1991 to 1996 would be counted as pensionable time; employees who did not have Croatian citizenship were guaranteed temporary work permits; employees with disabilities were guaranteed the right to a pension and employees whose present jobs were no longer required were guaranteed the right to retrain for other positions.

Reintegration of local Postal and Telephone departments was in its final stages.

The Joint Implementation Committee (JIC) on Public Utilities organized meetings between local employees and representatives of Croatian management and the Regional Executive Council to address concerns of employees regarding future employment. A meeting between HPT managers and representatives of the local PTT was held in Vukovar. Both sides agreed on specific positions to be offered to the nearly 400 employees of PTT. It was agreed that work contracts would be distributed early in March.

Voter registration for elections

If you were a 1991 resident of the Region, you did not need to complete a voter registration form as your name on the 1991 census put you on the voters list. It was essential that all displaced persons in the Region complete a voter's registration form at one of the UNTAES document centers (UDCs) so that voting facilities could be provided.

a. If you arrived in the Region after 1991 but before January 15, 1996, from another part of Croatia, you could register to vote when applying for your documents. You had to indicate whether you wanted to vote for local bodies in the Region or for local bodies in the place of your former residence. If you did not indicate your choice, your name remained on the voter's lists in the municipality where you lived in 1991. You could then vote only in that municipality.

b. If you had already obtained your citizenship papers and identification card, you had to again go to the UDC to complete the voter registration form and indicate your choices.

c. If you arrived in the Region after January 15, 1996 from another part of Croatia, your name remained on the voters list in the munici-pality where you lived in 1991 and you could only vote for that mu-nicipality. People had to register by March 21 to ensure that they could vote in the election.

We began to explain, in detail, how the election process would pro-ceed, who would be considered for elections, etc. There was a great deal for the people to learn and a lot of effort went into educating them. I remember producing videos every day, writing articles for the daily publication that was printed in Serbian, Croatian and English, so that the UNTAES staff could also understand what was happening. We used Koffi Annan's photograph wherever we could, since he had just taken over at the U.N. It seemed to be reassuring to the populace. Of course…that was a long time ago.

CHAPTER 19

VUKOVAR ELECTIONS BEGIN

<u>A message from UN Secretary General Koffi Annan</u>

Vote for your future on April 13th

<u>Who will conduct the elections?</u>

The actual conduct of the elections in each municipality was the responsibility of Local Electoral Commissions (LECs) which had been
appointed by the Joint Implementation Committee (JIC) on Elections.
LECs were comprised of three members and three deputy members.
As a rule, two members were nominated by the Croatian delegation;

two by the Serb delegation and the remaining two were from minority groups. LECs had been appointed to each of the 28 municipalities with their seat of operations in the UNTAES Region. Two municipalities, Osijek and Nustar, had their seat of operations outside the Region but had portions of territory within the Region. The Croatian Government has appointed LECs for these two.

Who was to be elected in the forthcoming elections?

In the elections of April 13, 1997, the citizens of Croatia elected their representatives as members of representational bodies of the local self-government units:

-- Members of the municipal councils elected by citizens of municipalities;

-- Members of the city councils elected by citizens of cities;

-- Members of the county assemblies elected by all citizens of counties; and

-- Representatives to the House of Counties of the Parliament of the Republic of Croatia elected by all citizens of Croatia in such a way those citizens of each county elected three representatives.

What is the mandate of the bodies being elected?

By the Act of Local Self-government, Municipal Councils had the authority to:

-- Ensure conditions to maintain public facilities, town planning and protecting the environment

-- Taking care of arranging settlements, quality of living conditions, communal facilities, communal and other public services and local infrastructure

-- Ensure meeting the local needs of the residents in the field of childcare, education and culture, public health (clinics and hospitals)

-- Organize animal health care and plant protection, social care, culture, physical culture and sports and govern communal property.

City Councils had the authority to:

-- Carry out activities similar to those of community councils; and conduct all other activities, which were directly connected to the interests of the city

-- Community for economic, cultural and social progress

The County had the authority to:

-- Coordinate interests and conduct activities for the balanced economic and social progress of the municipalities and cities within a County as well as the County as a whole

-- Coordinate the viewpoints of communities and cities and solve issues of common interests

-- Coordinate progress of cultural, educational, social, and communal and other institutions as well as infrastructure of importance for the area of the County as a whole.

Who could vote?

Croatian citizens 18 years and older, those who have their residence on the territory of a Municipality, City, County for whose representational body the elections were being held and those who were listed on voters lists in their place of residence.

Every candidate for representational body had to meet four pre-conditions.

They had to be citizens of the Region under the Transitional Administration, providing they had their place of residence in parts of Osijek-Baranja County or Vukovar-Sirmium County, which were under the Transitional Administration at the time of the 1991 Census. They had to be listed on voter's lists and have the right to participate in local elections providing they fulfilled the above-mentioned pre-conditions.

Croatian citizens who were members of the Serb ethnic community and moved into the Region under Transitional Administration before the beginning of the UNTAES mandate (January 15, 1996), who lived in the Region and who did not have their place of residence in the Region at the time of the Census in 1991, could choose to vote either for:

■ Governmental bodies at their current address in the Region or

■ Local governmental bodies in the area of their place of residence as of 1991, in other parts of Croatia

How to cast your vote

First of all, check your name in the voter's list. Voter lists will be displayed outside every polling station in the Region.

What must you bring with you when you vote?

210

You should bring with you any of the following identification documents:

-- **A** new Croatian ID; or

-- A valid Croatian Passport

How does the voting process work?

When you come in, you will first see the line controller who controls the access to the polling place.

The ID officer of the Polling Station Committee will verify identity by checking one of the approved personal documents:

-- Your new Croatian ID; or

-- Your valid Croatian Passport

The officer will then verify your name on the voters' list and then direct you to the member who will give you the ballot papers.

The member who gives out the ballot papers will give you five of them.

There will be five ballot papers in five different colors (Pink, Brown, Blue, White and Purple) and five appropriate ballot boxes at each polling station.

The ballot paper for the party list of candidates for the election of the House of Counties of the Croatian Parliament will be PINK.

The ballot paper for the election of individual candidates for County Assembly will be BROWN.

The ballot paper for the party list of candidates for election for the County Assembly will be BLUE.

The ballot paper for the election of individual candidates for the Municipal or City Council will be WHITE.

The ballot paper for the party list of candidates for the Municipal or City Council will be PURPLE.

What comes next?

After taking the ballot papers you should go to one of the voting booths. Draw a circle around the number in front of the party name or candidate for whom you want to vote. Mark only one number on each ballot paper with a pen provided for that purpose. Before you step out of the voting booth, fold each ballot paper in half.

Put each ballot paper carefully into the ballot box marked with the appropriate copy of the ballot paper on the outside of the box.

A person who cannot write, or a person with a physical challenge, not in a position to vote because of blindness, a physical disorder or illiteracy, can come to the polling station with another person who is literate. That person will be authorized to mark the ballot papers on behalf of the voter.

The representatives of parties or candidates (observers) have the right to observe the voting procedure. For all questions they must contact the chairman of the polling station.

The members of the electoral committees were:

-- The chairman

-- The deputy chairman

-- Four other committee members (two members and two deputy members)

Your vote is secret. Therefore, the polling place will be arranged in such a way that no one will be able to see how you mark your ballot paper.

Monitoring

UNTAES set up an Election Operations Center in the elections unit office in Vukovar Headquarters, which received all observer reports within and outside the Region. UNTAES and other international observers monitored the entire voting and counting process on an around-the-clock basis. The United States embassy made available more than 40 observers who observed the absentee voting process in 48 locations outside of the Region. A large number of mobile and static observers from the Organization of Security and Cooperation in Europe (OSCE) also participated in the monitoring.

Municipalities and Cities in the two Counties

50 Polling Stations were set up in the following locations:

Osijek-Baranja County:

1. Antunovac: Antunovac.

2. Beli Manastir: Beli Manastir, Branjii Vrh, Secerana and Sumarina.

3. Bilje: Bilje, Kopacevo, Kozjak, Lug Podunavlje, Tikves, Vardarac and Zlatn Greda.

4. Ceminac: Ceminac, Grabovac, Kozaral and Mitrovac.

5. Darda: Darda, Mece, Svajcernica and Ugljes.

6. Draz; Draz, Batina, Dubosevica, Gajic Podolje and Topolje.

7. Erdut: Erdut, Aljmas, Bijelo Brdo and Dalj.

8. Ernestinovo: Ernestinovo, Divos and Laslovo.

9. Jagodnjak: Jagodnjak, Majske Medje Bolman, Novi Bolman and Novi Ceminac

10. Knezevi Vinogradi: Knezevi Vinogra. di, Jasenovac, Kamenac, Karanac, Kotlina Mirkovac, Sokolovac, Sola and Zmajevac

11. Petlovac: Petlovac, Baranjsko Petrovc Selo, Luc, Novo Nevesinje, Novi Bezdan, Sirine, Sudaraz, Torjanci and Zeleno Polje.

12. Popovac: Popovac, Knezevo and Branjina.

13. Sodolovci: Sodolovci, Koprivna, Petrova Slatina, Paulin Dvor, Ada, Palaca and Silas.

14. Tenja: Tenja.

15. Osijek: Klisa and Sarvas.

Vukovar-Sirmium County:

1. Bogdanovci: Bogdanovci,Petrovci Svinjarevci.

2. Borovo: Borovo Selo:

3. llok: llok, Sarengrad, Mohovo and Bapsl

4. Lovas: Lovas and Opatovac.

5. Markusica: Markusica, Podrinje, Gab Ostrovo and Karadzicevo.

6. Mirkovci: Mirkovci.

7. Negoslavci: Negoslavci.

8. Nijemci: Nijemci, Sidski Banovci, Vi kovacki Banovci, Djeletovci, Donje No' Selo, Podgradje, Apsevci and Lipovac.

9. Nustar: Ceric and Marinci.

10. Stari Jankovci: Stari Jankovci, No Jankovci, Srijemske Laze, Slakovci and Orolik.

11. Tompojevci: Tompojevci, Miklusevi Grabovo, Cakovci, Boksic and Berak.

12. Tordinci: Tordinci, Mlaka Antins, Antin and Korodj.

13. Tovarnik: Tovarnik and llaca.

14. Trpinja: Trpinja, Bobota, Brsadi Pacetin, Ludvinci, Celije and Vera.

15. Vukovar: Vukovar, Borovo Nasel~ Jakobovac, Lipovaca, Ovcara, Solin aJ Luzac.

Counting of votes:

After closing of the polling stations at 7:00 P.M., the Chairman of the Polling Station Committee, in the presence of the UNTAES observers, all the members of this committee, party and candidate representatives and national observers, sealed the ballot boxes. The number of voters was determined and recorded as well as the number of the unused ballot papers. The ballot boxes were then opened for the ballot papers to be counted. Counting began immediately upon the conclusion of voting and had to be completed within 12 hours. The number of votes for each list of party candidates was determined first, followed by the number of votes of individual candidates. That data was recorded and sent to the relevant Local Electoral Committee. Three members of the local electoral committee (LEC) had to sign the results.

Absentee Voting

UNTAES made arrangements for absentee voting at all the polling stations in the Region. Those Displaced Persons (DPs) who moved to the Region after 1991 but before January 15, 1996, from other parts of Croatia, who were registered as voters and opted to vote for their original place of residence could vote at the polling stations within the Region. Absentee voters in the Region voted for about 85 different municipalities in other parts of Croatia.

Absentee voters had to go to a designated Absentee Polling Station, which was nearest to the place where they were currently living.

The Croatian Government also made arrangements to establish polling stations in about 75 locations throughout Croatia for DPs from the Region who were currently living in other parts of Croatia. Results from these absentee-voting stations outside the Region were communicated to the relevant local electoral commissions (LECs). UN and international observers monitored all voting locations.

Political Parties in the Fray

The following political parties participated in the elections:

(HDZ) Croatian Democratic Union

(HKDU) Croatian Christian Democratic Union

(HNS) Croatian People's Party

(HSLS) Croatian Social Liberal Party

(HSP) Croatian Party of Rights

(HSP-1861) Croatian Party of Rights -1861

(HSS) Croatian Peasants Party

(SBHS) Croatian Party of Slavonija and Baranja

(SDP) Social Democratic Party of Croatia

(SDSS) Independent Democratic Serb Party

Other candidates included those representing the Hungarian community, as well as several hundred independent candidates.

CHAPTER 20

A SUCCESSFUL CONCLUSION

UNTAES played its part effectively and admirably and all members of the UNTAES mission…civilian and military, local and international… should be congratulated for their commitment and contribution to a peaceful transition in Eastern Slavonia.

This was a remarkable story of the UNTAES mission and its contributions to the peaceful reintegration of the Eastern Slavonian region into the Republic of Croatia. Few could have expected when the mission began back in the depths of the winter 1996 that it would have achieved so much. It was a unique UN mission that combined traditional peacekeeping with demilitarization and peace enforcing, as well as a major humanitarian and political effort to help the Region's civilian population recover from a senseless and brutal war.

There were still several months to go before the mandate was completed but a solid bedrock of work had ensured that a positive end-of-mission would be seen in January 1998. The achievements of UNTAES would not have been possible without the hard work and commitment of the men and women, military and civilian, from around the world who participated in its unique work.

The military component of UNTAES, the United Nations Transitional Administration of Eastern Slavonia, Baranja, and Western Sirmium was comprised of approximately 5,000 troops. Various contingents from 10 different nations including Belgium, Russia, Pakistan, Jordan, Argentina, Ukraine, Slovakia, Poland, Indonesia, and The Czech Republic came together bringing their culture, religion and values to the Region.

To Bring the Region together, retain its multi-ethnic character and to promote an atmosphere of confidence among all local residents, irrespective of their ethnic origin, was our goal. To enable refugees and displaced persons to enjoy the right of return freely to their homes and to live there in conditions of security was another goal. To promote respect for the highest standards of human rights and fundamental freedoms and promote redevelopment and reconstruction of the Region in harmony with the Republic of Croatia was a third goal.

We wanted people to work together, build trust and break down the fear and hatred that had developed during more than four years of war. In the autumn of 1996, this process bore fruit when Belgrade and Zagreb established diplomatic ties and mutually recognized each other as fully sovereign and independent states.

Eastern Slavonia In 1991

In the spring of 1991 Eastern Slavonia, Baranja and Western Sirmium had a population of some 190,000 people drawn from a variety of ethnic backgrounds: 45% Croats, 25% Serbs, and the remainder Yugoslavs, Hungarians, Czechs, Gypsies, Italians, Muslims, Ruthenians, Slovaks and Ukrainians.

The Croat declaration of independence from the then Socialist Federal Republic of Yugoslavia and the subsequent armed response by ethnic Serbs, turned the region into a bloody battlefield. Local Serb forces backed by the Yugoslav National Army seized control of the region. Croat forces held out in Vukovar for over 100 days before surrendering in November 1991 but the city was devastated in the battle. Few buildings were untouched by some of the worst fighting in Europe since World War Two. Neighbors fought neighbors in brutal ethnic warfare. An estimated 80,000 refugees fled into Croatia and several thousand more ended up in Yugoslavia and Hungary.

A tense military stand off then continued until 1995, with forces of the locally recruited Serb forces, the so-called Army of Republic Serb Krajina (ARSK), occupying the Region and large Croatian forces massed across the frontline. Skirmishes and incidents between the two forces were a regular occurrence.

1995 -A Changed Strategic Situation: The Defeat of the Krajina Serbs

The first area to fall to the reinvigorated Croatian military was Western Slavonia, termed by the UN as Sector West, after a three-day offensive in May. Three months later Operation Storm was launched, which defeated the Krajina Serb forces in the UN Sector South and North. More than a hundred thousand Serbs fled into Bosnia and then into Yugoslavia. Eastern Slavonia looked like the next objective of the triumphant Croatian army.

The Basic Agreement of November 12, 1995

To head off an all-out Croatian offensive that may have sparked intervention by Federal Yugoslav military forces in neighboring Serbia, the International Contact Group including France, Germany, Russia, the United Kingdom and the United States sponsored talks between the Croatian Government and the local Serb leadership in Eastern Slavonia. It worked and a basic agreement was decided upon.

The First Success for UNTAES

In January 1996, Eastern Slavonia was the base for between 8,000 and 12,000 armed Serb soldiers of the Army of Republic Serb Krajina ('ARSK'), 11 Slavonia Baranja Corps and a number of small nationalist Serb Para-military militias. These included the notorious warlord Arkan and his Tiger militia, as well as two other groups called the Scorpions and Jumping Snakes. Almost every able-bodied adult male was serving in some form of military or paramilitary group. Lack of discipline and drunkenness were rife. Civilians and UN personnel were often attacked and robbed as they went about their daily business.

One of UNTAES' first missions was to negotiate and then implement the demilitarization of the Region to restore respect for the UN and provide a secure environment for the return of normality and peace. Between January and May 1996, UNTAES, under then Force Commander Major General Jozef Schoups, of Belgium, began to build up its military forces from 1,600 lightly armed peacekeepers to 5,000 peace enforcers, backed by 50 tanks, 204 armored vehicles, 21 mortars, 12 artillery pieces, six assault and six transport helicopters and NATO air power. Close links were established with NATO's Peace Implementation Force (IFOR) in Bosnia-Herzegovina. Contingency plans were prepared for IFOR to come to the assistance of UNTAES in emergencies and these links were retained when IFOR handed over to its successor, the Stabilization Force (SFOR) in December 1996. Liaison and communication links were opened with NATO's 5th Allied Tactical Air Force (5 ATAF) in Italy to ensure the quick provision of close air support for UNTAES in a crisis. UNTAES tactical air control parties conducted weekly training with NATO aircraft operating over the Region. In May, the demilitarization process formally began with the majority of the ARSK's 120 tanks,120 artillery pieces, 140 mortars and other heavy weapons being taken out of the region to Yugoslavia. The ARSK then disbanded itself and its former soldiers became civilians en masse.

To the south of Vukovar, Serb Para-militaries from the Scorpions were not as co-operative as the mainstream ARSK units and refused to participate in the demilitarization process. On May 14th, UNTAES troops, tanks and artillery from its Jordanian battalion backed by Ukrainian MI-24 assault helicopters were deployed in a show of strength to force the Scorpions to leave their base at the Djeletovci oil fields. UNTAES chief of staff Belgian Colonel Jean-Marie Jockin gave them an ultimatum. "We would like to do this peacefully. It's up to you". Within a short time the Scorpions were heading for the Yugoslav border in a fleet of 150 cars. Others fled into the countryside on foot. A month later Arkan's Tigers vacated their base in Erdut and went to Yugoslavia.

By June 21st the process of demilitarization was formally declared over and UNTAES was the sole military force in the region. It however was mandated to preserve the demilitarized status of the region and acted to do so on a number of occasions, against both Serb and Croat infringements. Between July 19 and 26, 1996 a strong group of Croatian Special Policemen entered the demilitarized zone, which defined the area between Croatian government control and the area that had been administered by UNTAES. Four of the policemen were detained and disarmed by Belgian Para-Commandos. They were eventually returned to Croatian controlled territory.

Weapons Buy-back Program

Although the demilitarization removed all the heavy weapons from the Region, it did not deal with the large numbers of small arms held by almost every adult. To take as many arms out of circulation as possible, UNTAES began a weapons buy-back program on October 2, 1996. In return for cash payments funded by the Croatian government some 4,690 rifles, 4,620 disposable and 590 reusable rocket launchers, 11,760 grenades and 971,000 rounds of ammunition were handed into UNTAES collection points by April 30, 1997.

Beginning in May of 1996, Eastern Slavonia was transformed into a largely peaceful region. On December 3rd, 1996, Croatian President Franjo Tudjman made his historic visit to Vukovar, hosted by UNTAES. In the wake of the successful demilitarization campaign, UNTAES put increasing emphasis on its efforts to move along the political process to re-integrate the Region into the Republic of Croatia. This was done in the face of political and rhetorical opposition from nationalist groups on both sides of the old frontline.

UNTAES Rebuilds a Society

UNTAES had the unprecedented mission of peacefully bringing together a number of very distinct ethnic groups into a single democratic
society. This was far from being an easy task. Many local people had
little understanding of democratic processes or the rule of law. Others
were unaware of Croatian legal and constitutional procedures. Others
had swallowed years of war propaganda and could not bring themselves to have any contact whatsoever with what they saw as the 'enemy' state. UNTAES political, civil and public affairs components,
alongside UNTAES military personnel and civilian police, guided, assisted and educated Eastern Slavonia's population towards the goal of
re-integration into the Republic of Croatia.

UNTAES efforts were aimed at enabling the local Serbs to take full
advantage of the legal rights they would gain as Croatian citizens to
enable them and their political leaders to play a full part in the countries political, administrative and social institutions. At every opportunity UNTAES stressed that only by early political and social engagement with Croatia would the people of the Region be able to preserve
their distinct cultural and political identity. Participation in the political
system would allow the local Serbs to retain control or influence in
vital local and regional government bodies. A major UNTAES initiative was the establishment of the Transitional Police Force (TPF),
made up at first of some 1,200 Serb, 400 Croat and other ethnic
groups, to police the region in an even handed manner. The TPF operated under the oversight of the UNTAES Civilian Police component,
which provided training and advice. We funded training programs, allowing them to operate using international standards. Other UNTAES
Civilian Police helped families trace missing relatives from the war
and assisted the Hague International War Crimes Tribunal investigate
alleged war crimes.

Along the Region's international borders, UNTAES border monitors
helped the TPF and Transitional Border Control Force, to operate customs and immigration procedures using recognized standards. Croatian
local government officials were brought into the Region by UNTAES

to help prepare for a smooth transition of town and county administrations into the country's system of government. School curriculum and qualifications were harmonized and multi-lingual certificates issued. The pension systems for old people and war widows was brought into line with those of Croatia, in a way that ensured the needy continued to receive support. Postal, telecommunications, public utilities and banking regulations were also prepared for re-integration.

The recasting of the Region's local government and administration had to go hand in hand with practical moves to remove the psychological barriers between people who had recently been waging ethnic warfare against each other.

UNTAES established an active public affairs component to get its message out to people who had previously been fed a daily diet of ethnic hatred and propaganda in local newspapers, television and radio reports. The UNTAES Bulletin was published bi-weekly and the mission produced daily television and radio programs for broadcast on its own transmitters.

From the start of the mission, UNTAES sought to break down the old frontlines to allow people free movement. A weekly market was started in August 1996 on a road in the zone of separation near Osijek, where some 140,000 people from all over the former Yugoslavia gathered to buy and sell goods or meet friends and relatives. When the telephone links to Croatia were switched back on 20,000 people made calls in the first 48 hours. In the UNTAES sponsorship program, more than 30,000 people were able to make visits across the old frontline. A temporary postal system was also set up so people could mail items to and from the Region.

UNTAES had a program of opening roads and bus routes throughout the Region for civilian traffic, including the main highway between Belgrade and Zagreb. All activities were closely controlled and monitored by UNTAES to ensure security.

Bringing People Together

More than four years of war left terrible scars on the landscape of Eastern Slavonia. The city of Vukovar needed almost total rebuilding. Few dwellings or industrial premises in the city were untouched in the 1991 battle. Numerous villages in the surrounding countryside were also devastated in the fighting. UNTAES headed up efforts to physically re-construct the Region and its economy. The two areas were closely linked, with economic activity at low levels and 65% of the adult male population unemployed. Agriculture was the only industry operating at anything like pre-war levels.

De-mining

During the war some 800,000 mines were laid on the battlefields of Eastern Slavonia and up to 100,000 unexploded munitions littered the Region's buildings, streets and fields. These posed a grave danger to the Region's inhabitants, seriously inhibiting its economic regeneration and the safe return of displaced persons to their former homes in frontline areas. The residue of war constantly injured civilians and livestock. UNTAES began to coordinate a program of de-mining in the Region, with its engineering experts helping to identify both sides' minefields from old records, where they still existed. Local and Croatian mine clearing companies, often made up of former military engineers, were contracted by international agencies and the Croatian Government to begin de-mining operations in a number of areas. This was a highly labor intensive, time consuming and expensive effort. It took one de-miner a whole day to clear 30 square yards. To date, thousand of mines have been cleared but conservative estimates expect the work to take up to 10 years to complete. UNTAES worked hard to promote international support for de- mining and attracted funding to the Region for this vital work from the UNHCR and European Union.

New Politics in Eastern Slavonia

On April 13, 1997 the political landscape of Eastern Slavonia was fundamentally transformed when the Region took part in Croatian town, county and parliamentary elections for the first time. Serb political parties contested the elections, which coincided with those taking place throughout Croatia. Croatian and Serbian politicians and parties stood against each other in a free and fair election, coordinated and monitored by the UNTAES Electoral Unit. The Transitional Administrator certified them as being up to international standards. The Region participated in Croatian Presidential elections later that same year. More than 100,000 local residents collected Croatian passports and identity papers at UNTAES organized document issue centers. Adults were then eligible to vote in the election. Within 30 days of the election, the Region's new political leaders assumed their posts. The UNTAES mandate continued until January 1998, with mission personnel and some military units remaining in the Region to monitor compliance with International agreements and treaties, along with continued upholding of international standards of human rights. The Security Council decided on the precise nature of the final six months mandate.

International engagement in the Region continued after the end of the UNTAES mandate with the proposed establishment of an Organization for Security and Cooperation in Europe (OSCE) monitoring mission. This substantial mission was tasked with monitoring the Croatian Government's compliance with human rights and other agreements.

"We can't change the past but we can build a future"

UNTAES created a framework for peace in the Region and contributed to the broader peace in the Balkans. Its presence and work on the ground served as a bridge for mutual recognition by Croatia and the Federal Republic of Yugoslavia. The credibility of the UNTAES mission brought much needed stability to that relationship.

An outbreak of violence in the region would have pushed the whole of the peace process in the former Yugoslavia back years and possibly sparked a major war. Our success at UNTAES contributed to peace and stability in Bosnia- Herzegovina.

The foundations were laid for a smooth transition to Croatian authorities during the final months of the mission. Then the OSCE arrived to set up a long term monitoring mission.

UNTAES worked to ensure the Region's demilitarized status continued after the end of the mandate as an anchor of stability for all of former Yugoslavia. So-called soft border controls with Yugoslavia allowed relatively free movement across the border, as well as the option of dual nationality for residents, were issues UNTAES pursued to help ease the transition to Croatian control.

The UNHCR refugee return program oversaw perhaps the greatest threat to the Region's peaceful future. This addressed the issue of refugee returns throughout Croatia, not just in the Region. The real test came when Croatians returned to live side by side with Serbs in Vukovar. People were encouraged to look forward not backwards.

Local leaders had to act quickly enough to take advantage of the new Croatian political system and structure. Now, the Region looked forward to a peaceful and prosperous future as part of a new democratic Croatia that was part of a democratic Europe.

-30-